Mark Balnaves is Program Director of the Bachelor of Social Science at the University of Queensland. An expert in survey methodology, he is the author of *Introduction to Quantitative Research Methods: An Investigative Approach*. He has also published on social equity and telecommunications, the sociology of information, social psychology methodology, and has produced multimedia courseware on descriptive statistics.

James Donald is Professor of Media and Head of the School of Media and Information at Curtin University of Technology, Western Australia. He is author of *Sentimental Education: Schooling, Popular Culture and the Regulation of Liberty* and *Imagining the Modern City*, and has edited a dozen books on the media, education and social theory. He edited the journal *Screen Education* and founded *New Formations*.

Stephanie Hemelryk Donald is Senior Lecturer in Media and Communication at the University of Melbourne. She is the author of *Public Secrets, Public Spaces: Cinema and Civility in China* and co-author of *The State of China Atlas*. She has co-edited *Belief in China: Art and Politics, Deities and Mortality; Picturing Power in the People's Republic of China: Posters of the Cultural Revolution;* and *Media in China: Content, Consumption and Crisis*.

Also in this series:

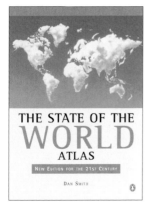

THE STATE OF THE WORLD ATLAS
6th edition
Dan Smith

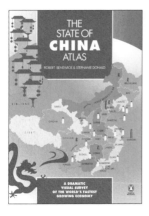

THE STATE OF CHINA ATLAS
Robert Benewick
and Stephanie Donald

THE PENGUIN ATLAS OF
HUMAN SEXUAL BEHAVIOR
Judith Mackay

THE PENGUIN ATLAS OF
MEDIA AND INFORMATION

Mark Balnaves, James Donald and
Stephanie Hemelryk Donald

PENGUIN REFERENCE

Penguin Putnam Inc., 375 Hudson Street,
New York, New York 10014, USA
Penguin Books Canada Limited, 10 Alcorn
Avenue, Toronto, Ontario, Canada M4V

Penguin Books Limited, Registered Offices:
Harmondsworth, Middlesex, England

First published 2001
10 9 8 7 6 5 4 3 2 1

Penguin Reference paperback 0 14 20.0017 5

Produced for the Penguin Group by
Myriad Editions Limited
6–7 Old Steine, Brighton BN1 1EJ, UK
www.MyriadEditions.com

Edited and co-ordinated for Myriad Editions
by Jannet King and Candida Lacey

Design and graphics by Corinne Pearlman
Maps created by Isabelle Lewis

Printed and bound in Hong Kong
Produced by Phoenix Offset Limited under the
supervision of The Hanway Press, London

CONTENTS

Remember back, if you can, to 1984. The year carried with it all the cultural connotations of George Orwell's dystopian novel *Nineteen Eighty-Four*. From the perspective of a depressed England recovering from World War II in the late 1940s, Orwell imagined a future totalitarian society that lived under the intimidating slogan "Big Brother Is Watching You". In this nightmarish world, television not only spewed a stream of propaganda into people's homes, it also acted as a medium of surveillance, recording the population's most intimate and mundane activities. When the actual year rolled around, there was some relief that Orwell's more extreme fears had proved unfounded, and even some optimism that the effect of the mass media in the totalitarian regimes of East and Central Europe was to provoke the desire for a vigorous civil society and alternative ways of life rather than docile conformity.

Looking back from the beginning of a new century, though, we can now see that 1984 was in some ways a revolutionary year. Although almost a decade since Paul Allen and Bill Gates had developed a BASIC computer language for the Altair 8800, 1984 was just three years after the MS-DOS operating system was introduced on the IBM Personal Computer. It was only a couple of years after the telecommunications industry had been deregulated in the USA and the UK, blurring the boundaries and barriers between the media, communication and information industries and so helping to create the conditions for a transformed economy. As an emblematic moment that stands for many of the changes in the world of media and information mapped in this book, however, consider this. During the half-time break in the television transmission of the 1984 American Super Bowl, a 45-second advertisement was screened – just once. It cost US$1.6 million to produce. It was directed by UK-born Ridley Scott, whose credits include *Alien*, *Blade Runner*, *Thelma and Louise*, *Gladiator* and *Hannibal*. Although Scott claims to have discovered "what it was we were selling" only at the end of the shoot, this was the entry of Apple Computers onto the world stage.

Dates and events like these provide a myth of origin for the idea that we have entered into an entirely new Information Age, radically different from what went before. That makes a good story. It is one that can be – and has been – told in terms of how Microsoft's marketing genius and aggression later saw the technologically superior but less savvy Apple struggling while Bill Gates became the world's richest man. (At one point Gates was richer than half the US population put together.) But it is important to disentangle what is genuinely new and different in the post-1980s era from the hype of gurus and hucksters, and also to record continuities from the past. This atlas is our attempt to do just that. It represents a snapshot of an exceptional moment. It is still informed by the old justification for the systematic academic study of the media: that looking at the institutions, practices and products of cinema, radio and television provides unique insights into the symbolic structures and political economy of modern societies, into the ideological aspects of the exercise of power, and into the profoundly mediated nature of the way we live together and of our inner life and experience. Now, however, many of us formed in the traditions of media studies in the second half of the 20th century are learning not just to address new phenomena but also to reconstruct previously neglected narratives that help us to understand a new media world.

There is nothing new about the economic importance of the media and communication, as demonstrated by the huge impact of the film and television industries in the last century. What is emerging as a result of the technological convergence between computers and telecommunications, however, are corporations that attempt to control both the infrastructure of delivery (telephone lines, fiber-optic cable, terrestrial and satellite television signals) and the content delivered (films, programs, texts, Web pages, databases, educational materials, or data on corporations, governments and individuals). The merger between America Online and Time Warner is just the most visible symbol of this development. The economic, social and cultural importance of content remains the same. The change in the medium of delivery, however, is of more than incidental importance. It brings the history of the person-to-person communication technologies that started with the telephone – which used to make an appearance only in more technologically oriented media histories – much more to the center of the story.

We now see that the media were always about allowing access to certain types of information and experience – stock market reports, news of world events, ideas, titillating stories, fantasies of escape into alternative worlds. They produced "immaterial commodities". Access and immateriality are key elements in an increasingly "weightless" economy that some analysts see emerging in the overdeveloped world: that is, an economy in which value is generated from control of content and from the technological pathways to that content.

What do such developments mean for the political and social functions attributed to the mass media of the 20th century? Newspapers and public service broadcasting were supposed to provide a forum for the dissemination of disinterested information and rational argument so that citizens could collectively reflect on issues of communal importance – the media as public sphere. Of course, the media have always had to attract paying customers and advertisers, they have routinely served party or sectional interests, and the profession of journalism can boast more than its fair share of scoundrels and timeservers. Even so, the importance of free and vigorous media to an effectively functioning democracy should not be underestimated. Some enthusiasts believe that the Internet will allow both global and local discussion without the intervention of partisan proprietors or national regulators. This pious hope was always based on too rosy an image of the future, which does justice neither to the nature of the new technology, nor to the complexities of individual participation in the formation of public opinion. Although the Internet has been used effectively by lobbyists, protest groups and the forces arrayed against globalization, an increasing number of gatekeepers are controlling – and charging for – access to information. To an unprecedented extent, information itself is becoming a commodity.

The "virtual" texture of individual experience and imaginative life has likewise been intensified. As early as 1916, the philosopher and psychologist Hugo Munsterberg noted how the then comparatively new medium of cinema enabled people to enjoy the experience of being simultaneously both "here" and "elsewhere". Eight decades later, in 1997, the editor of the *New York Times Book Review*, Charles McGrath recorded how the Internet can produce a vertiginous experience of an excess of information from elsewhere:

> A couple of weeks ago, during a long afternoon surfing the Internet, I experienced an overload. First I checked my e-mail messages (messages from the kids, from a former colleague setting up a lunch date and from someone in an electronic discussion group I joined a few months ago, talking about the Battle of Trafalgar). Then I read some valuable tips on lock-picking written by someone named Ted the Tool. I browsed through the various on-line journals – Slate, Salon, HotWired, Suck, Feed and Swoon. I consulted a weather map customized for my neighbourhood. I visited the poetry archive at the University of Toronto and ran a little search on the number of times the word "thistle" turns up in Byron. I stopped by the Kraft Interactive Kitchen and watched the dancing utensils for a while. I went to the Timothy Leary Home Page and read some of the gibberish posted there by fans of the late doctor. I also went to the Internet cemetery, a place where people leave testimonials to their departed loved ones.

Charles McGrath's experience may strike a chord with many readers of this book, however restricted it may be to a minority of people in the richer parts of the world.

Certainly, it captures something of the way the authors of this atlas and their collaborators have all learned more about the possibilities, the distractions and the frustrations of trying to access reliable information from the Internet. The way in which the atlas has been produced may itself be symptomatic of the newness and the continuities of the era in which we live. When work began, the three authors were all based in Perth, Western Australia, working with an editorial team based in Brighton on the south coast of the UK. Although famous for being the most remote metropolitan center in the world, Perth is in the same time zone as Singapore, Kuala Lumpur, Hong Kong, Beijing, Taipei and Tokyo. Head west and the first land you will hit is Durban in South Africa. Head a little more north and you come to Sri Lanka and the Indian sub-continent. Almost as far to the east, across the wide brown land of Australia, are the metropolitan centers of Melbourne and Brisbane – where two of the authors will be based by the time the book is published – and Sydney. This physical geography is relevant insofar as it has taught two of the authors, recent migrants from the UK, a refreshingly dislocated new perspective on global media. In other ways, it is increasingly irrelevant. The logic of research is now a constant email conversation with fellow scholars around the world, and instant Internet access. The logic of publishing involves not just time-delay conversations between Australia and Brighton, but printing of the book in Hong Kong and simultaneous publication by different publishers, in the USA, the UK, France and Germany. This all sounds terribly globalized. What is strange is how, despite all that, it is still the reality of human communication with colleagues (even those we never meet) that gets us through the deadlines. And there is nothing new about that. As the 19th-century novelists used to say, it is the communication with you, dear virtual reader, that still makes us go through the painful process of creation.

For all that, it is important to insist again that Charles McGrath's glut of information and our globalized mode of production are the privilege of a very small proportion of the world's population. It is also worth noting, without making heavy weather of it, that any reader of this atlas is bound to be struck by the skewed and partial nature of the so-called globalization of the new media and information order. Although companies such as WorldSpace may be attempting to provide cheaper, power-efficient wireless and satellite services to nations lacking well-developed terrestrial service, this remains, economically and in terms of control over the majority of both content and infrastructure, an unequal world. It would take a George Orwell to do that story justice. Here we offer information and ideas from which you may construct your own analytical narratives and draw your own conclusions.

Mark Balnaves, James Donald,
Stephanie Hemelryk Donald
Australia, March 2001

ACKNOWLEDGEMENTS
The information in this atlas has been compiled from the sources listed in the References. The opinions in the text are those of the authors. The atlas does not purport to give any specific advice, and should not be taken or relied upon as doing so.

Here we would like to acknowledge people and organizations who have helped us with this project.

For expert advice on specific spreads:
    Matthew Allen, School of Media and
    Information, Curtin University;
    Ang Peng Hwa, Nanyang Technological
    University, Singapore;
    John Gammack, CECIS, Murdoch University;
    Paul Genoni, School of Media and
    Information, Curtin University;
    Jane Klobas, School of Media and
    Information, Curtin University;
    Mia Lindgren, Murdoch University Radio;
    Donna Robson, Westinfo;
    Trevor Sofield, University of Tasmania;
    Fay Sudweeks, CECIS, Murdoch University.

For research assistance and advice on tracing information:
    Tracey Crawcour; Kay Fisher; the library
    services of Murdoch University and the
    University of Queensland.

For financial support:
    Curtin University and the Australian
    Research Council for a Small Grant for
    research into media regulation;
    Murdoch University Division of Social
    Sciences, Humanities and Education Grants
    Scheme.

For editorial guidance, support, discipline and patience:
    Jannet King, Candida Lacey and Corinne
    Pearlman at Myriad Editions.

THE INFORMATION AGE

Subscriptions to Integrated Services Digital
Networks (ISDN), which allow high-speed
Internet and communications access,
grew from 3 million in 1995
to over 13 million in 2000.

THE INFORMATION SOCIETY

The last three decades of the 20th century saw dramatic changes in the way we live – an Information Revolution, some people call it.

In terms of technology, the Information Revolution refers to the possibilities opened up by digitization: the power of computers to store, manipulate and transmit information in the form of speech, data and video more compactly, more cheaply and at greater speed than ever before. This capacity enabled three previously separate industries – telecommunications, electronics (including the electronic media) and computing – to converge as a new juggernaut known as Information Technology, or IT. The variety, sophistication and sheer number of IT devices introduced into our working lives and our homes led to excited talk about entering a new Information Age, supposedly as radically different from the Industrial Age as that was from the agricultural societies that preceded it.

What has changed – economically, socially and culturally? Do the changes really represent an epochal shift? Has the technology caused the changes, or has its availability simply accelerated trends that were already underway? Will IT be as important historically as steam power or electricity were in the Industrial Revolution?

In economic terms, the most striking thing about IT has been the unprecedented coincidence of increasing power with falling costs. It took from the 1790s until 1850 for the price of steam power to halve. The price of electricity fell by 65 percent between 1890 and 1930, a decline of no more than 2 to 3 percent a year. In comparison, the price of computer processing power has fallen by an average of 30 percent a year over the past 20 years, and is now just 0.01 percent of its level in the early 1970s. This astonishing reduction in cost has accelerated the global spread of the "information highway".

New information and communication technologies have changed the way we work, allowing greater control over the processes of production and distribution. To what extent they have caused changes in the *type* of work we do is more debatable. In the advanced industrial nations the growth of IT has coincided with the growth of the service sector – an elastic category that can include anything from stock-broking, librarianship, computer maintenance or journalism to belly-dancing. Whether IT has *caused* this shift, which was already apparent in the USA in the 1950s (see right), is open to question. In countries such as China and Thailand, where nearly half the working population is still employed on the land, the transition is bound to be slower.

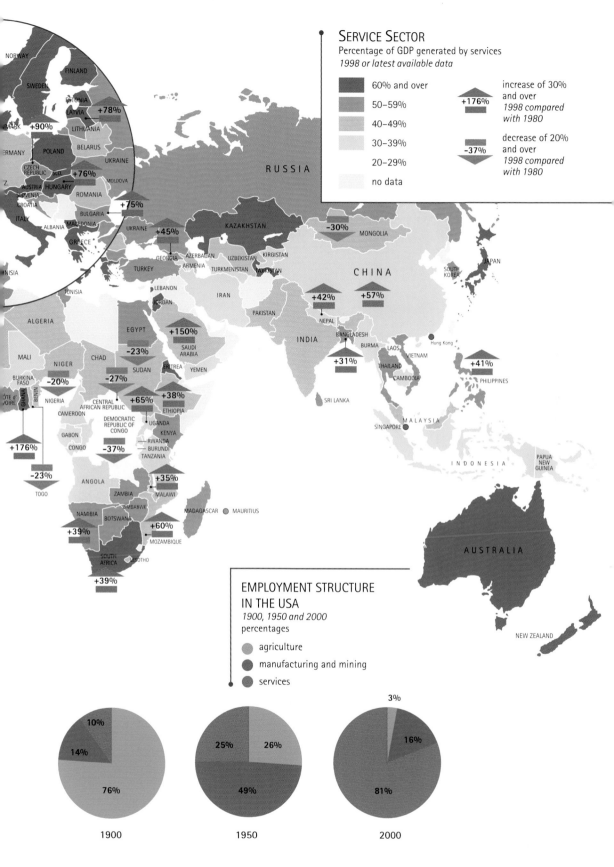

Map labels: NORWAY, FINLAND, SWEDEN, ESTONIA, LATVIA +78%, +90%, LITHUANIA, GERMANY, POLAND, BELARUS, CZECH REPUBLIC, UKRAINE, AUSTRIA, HUNGARY +76%, MOLDOVA, SLOVENIA, ROMANIA, CROATIA, BULGARIA +75%, ALBANIA, MACEDONIA, ITALY, GREECE, TUNISIA, RUSSIA, KAZAKHSTAN, MONGOLIA −30%, UKRAINE +45%, GEORGIA, AZERBAIJAN, ARMENIA, UZBEKISTAN, KIRGISTAN, TURKEY, TURKMENISTAN, TAJIKISTAN, LEBANON, JORDAN, IRAN, PAKISTAN, CHINA, SOUTH KOREA, JAPAN, ALGERIA, EGYPT +150%, −23%, SAUDI ARABIA, NEPAL +42%, +57%, INDIA, BANGLADESH +31%, BURMA, LAOS, Hong Kong, MALI, CHAD, SUDAN −27%, ERITREA, YEMEN, VIETNAM, THAILAND, CAMBODIA, +41%, PHILIPPINES, NIGER, BURKINA FASO −20%, CÔTE d'IVOIRE, GHANA, BENIN, NIGERIA, CENTRAL AFRICAN REPUBLIC +65%, +38%, ETHIOPIA, CAMEROON, +176%, DEMOCRATIC REPUBLIC OF CONGO −37%, UGANDA, KENYA, RWANDA, BURUNDI, SRI LANKA, GABON, CONGO, TANZANIA, SINGAPORE, MALAYSIA, −23%, TOGO, ANGOLA, ZAMBIA, MALAWI +35%, ZIMBABWE, MADAGASCAR, MAURITIUS, INDONESIA, PAPUA NEW GUINEA, NAMIBIA, BOTSWANA, +60%, MOZAMBIQUE, +39%, SOUTH AFRICA, LESOTHO, +39%, AUSTRALIA, NEW ZEALAND

EMPLOYMENT STRUCTURE IN THE USA
1900, 1950 and 2000
percentages

- agriculture
- manufacturing and mining
- services

1900: 10%, 14%, 76%

1950: 25%, 26%, 49%

2000: 3%, 16%, 81%

So far, instant global communications show few signs of producing an economically more equitable global society. Instead, since the world's great stock trading centers were linked together in the 1970s they have created a global financial market that is increasingly detached from the actual performance of national economies. Almost as spectacular has been the rise of information- and computer-based companies such as Microsoft, and the embarrassing fall of many small-to-medium ventures. Although a "dot com" a day was going bust towards the end of 2000, this did not altogether stop the flow of venture capital.

As for the social impact of the Information Revolution, although the sillier predictions that the Internet will kill off schools, libraries and hospitals are greatly exaggerated, the way those institutions operate is certainly changing. The much-hyped phenomenon of telecommuting – using computers and online facilities to work from home – is a new way of working being adopted mainly by some large organizations (see right). The proportion of companies allowing workers the option of telecommuting rose from 15 percent in 1995 to 28 percent in 1999. Although official estimates of how many US citizens telecommute range from 7 million (US Bureau of Labor Statistics) to nearly 20 million (International Telework Association and Council), sceptics are still to be convinced that the practice will become widespread. The really cynical suspect that more people are writing theses about it than are actually doing it.

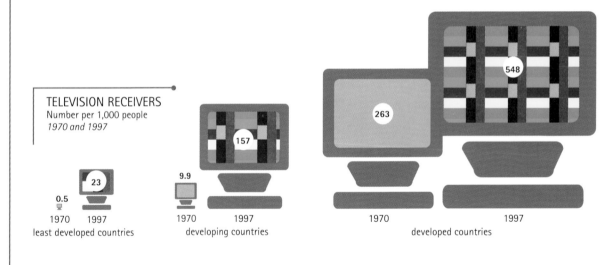

TELEVISION RECEIVERS
Number per 1,000 people
1970 and 1997

0.5 | 23
1970 | 1997
least developed countries

9.9 | 157
1970 | 1997
developing countries

263 | 548
1970 | 1997
developed countries

The efficiency of control and communication made possible by IT has no doubt contributed to the growth of multinational corporations, which now account for something like 20 percent of world production and 70 percent of world trade. The term "multinational" does not, of course, mean "owned by many nations". In terms of economic power, the Information Age, continues to be a nation-state affair. It looks more like a patchwork quilt than a global village.

In terms of culture, the industrial significance of the media and of entertainment will continue to grow, with profound consequences for the rhythm and dynamics of everyday life. The home will become even more a hub for leisure and entertainment activities, with an increased use of videos, video games, online shopping and the Internet. Television ownership in the world's poorer nations is growing, although it is still far below the level in richer countries (see above).

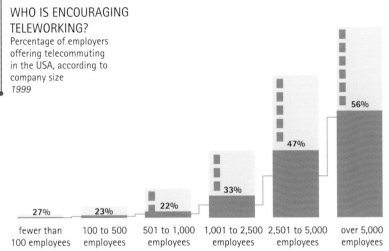

WHO IS ENCOURAGING TELEWORKING?
Percentage of employers offering telecommuting in the USA, according to company size
1999

fewer than 100 employees	100 to 500 employees	501 to 1,000 employees	1,001 to 2,500 employees	2,501 to 5,000 employees	over 5,000 employees
27%	23%	22%	33%	47%	56%

It is estimated that by 2004 the average citizen of the USA will devote more than ten hours a day, and spend $792 a year, in order to stay informed and entertained. By 2004, 67 million homes in the USA will be linked to the Internet – as many as now subscribe to cable television – and the average person will spend 187 hours a year online. The reliability of such speculations is always open to doubt. The tantalizing question is what sort of people we shall become, and what new forms of community we shall be able to sustain.

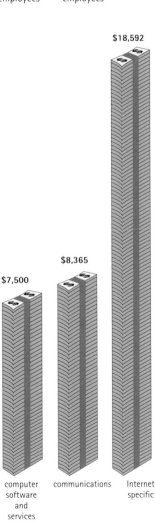

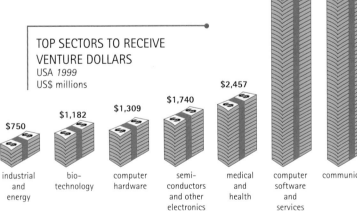

TOP SECTORS TO RECEIVE VENTURE DOLLARS
USA *1999*
US$ millions

industrial and energy	bio-technology	computer hardware	semi-conductors and other electronics	medical and health	computer software and services	communications	Internet specific
$750	$1,182	$1,309	$1,740	$2,457	$7,500	$8,365	$18,592

15

ACCESS TO IDEAS

Even in the new Information Age, some age-old questions still apply. Who has access to information? On what terms? How is information stored and managed?

The physical preservation of information became possible with the emergence of the written word. Writing, and later print, transformed social, cultural, political and economic life, and remain central to the latest information and communication technologies (ICTs). The integration of text with electronically reproduced images and sounds is at the heart of emerging new media.

Millions of people are still excluded from this brave new information world by the brute fact of illiteracy. Around 20 percent of the world's population and about 30 percent of women are illiterate. Education plays an important part in determining people's ability to access information and whether they can make productive use of it.

As the map shows, access to the information housed in public libraries varies enormously across the world. The Internet, for all its promise of universal access, is useless without a telephone line or a cable or wireless connection. Even for those with a telephone line and a computer, there are further barriers to overcome. Unless you speak English, most of the information available on the Internet will be meaningless – although other languages, such as Spanish and Chinese, are expected to be equally widespread by 2020.

The new ICTs have the capacity to make unprecedented quantities of information freely available. They are also being used to transform information into a commodity. Increasingly, we have to pay for access.

These technological and social developments are bringing about profound changes in the role and practices of two of the oldest professions in the world of information. For centuries archivists have preserved an accumulation of human knowledge in the form of books, documents and other media, to be retrieved by future generations. Librarians have had the responsibility of enabling scholars and other searchers to find the information they seek. The new technologies have created new possibilities for the storage, preservation and retrieval of information.

They have also opened up more entrepreneurial possibilities for these ancient professions. Today's archivists and librarians are tomorrow's information gatekeepers and knowledge managers.

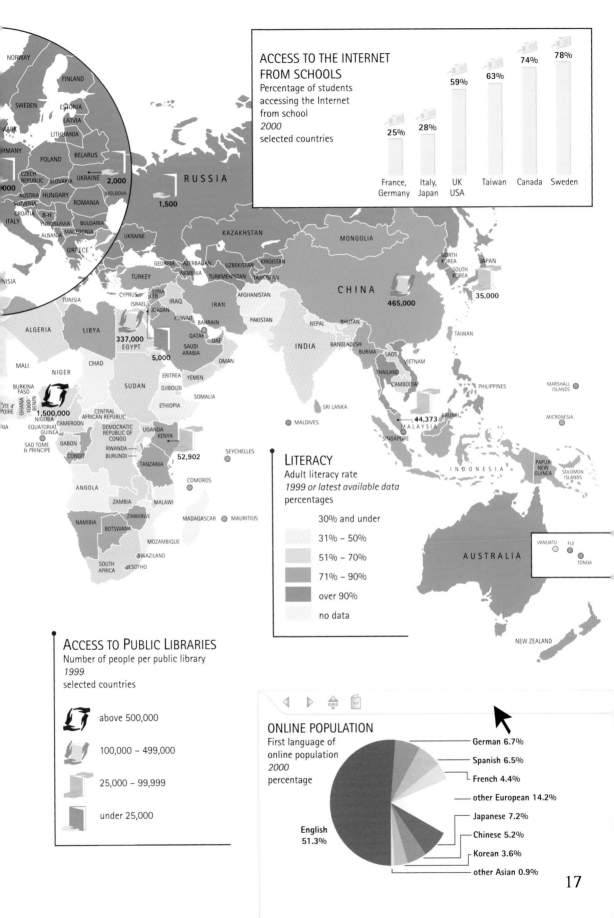

ACCESS TO THE INTERNET FROM SCHOOLS
Percentage of students accessing the Internet from school
2000
selected countries

France, Germany	Italy, Japan	UK USA	Taiwan	Canada	Sweden
25%	28%	59%	63%	74%	78%

LITERACY
Adult literacy rate
1999 or latest available data
percentages

- 30% and under
- 31% – 50%
- 51% – 70%
- 71% – 90%
- over 90%
- no data

ACCESS TO PUBLIC LIBRARIES
Number of people per public library
1999
selected countries

- above 500,000
- 100,000 – 499,000
- 25,000 – 99,999
- under 25,000

ONLINE POPULATION
First language of online population
2000
percentage

- English 51.3%
- German 6.7%
- Spanish 6.5%
- French 4.4%
- other European 14.2%
- Japanese 7.2%
- Chinese 5.2%
- Korean 3.6%
- other Asian 0.9%

17

E-COMMERCE

Shopping, banking and contacting the government online are all options available in the wired world. E-commerce (electronic commerce) and m-commerce (mobile commerce) are growing rapidly in B2B (business-to-business) transactions. This is a challenge for those nations and disadvantaged groups not yet able to access digital technology. Security is an important factor in customer confidence and nations without secure-server capability are unlikely to develop successful e-commerce trading. However, even secure servers are not enough to ensure that e-commerce flourishes. Delivery routes and local tastes are still major factors in e-tailing (electronic retailing) decisions, as evidenced by the decision in 2000 of the huge US company buy.com to pull out of Australia in order to concentrate on its domestic market.

Australia 1999
22% of small-to-medium enterprises connected to Internet were engaged in B2B e-commerce.

B2C (business-to-consumer) trading is also increasing in terms of volume sales, particularly in the USA, and to a lesser extent in parts of Asia and Western Europe. It offers many financial benefits for businesses. Paperwork is diminished when purchase orders and invoices are reconciled electronically, and packaging and postage costs are avoided by emailing to customers products such as airline tickets and software purchases. Warehousing in bulk is also cheaper than maintaining a high-street presence with a large storage facility on site, although most online consumers prefer to have a physical retail site where they can return faulty goods and meet representatives to discuss problems.

A website is a cheaper "salesperson" than an individual who has to move from one potential customer to another, sometimes with a low success rate. Although there are factors such as consumer trust, individual loyalty to a representative, and the sheer face-to-face charm a trained salesperson can provide and

WHY BANKS LIKE INTERNET DELIVERY
Cost per transaction by method of delivery US$

$0.01	$0.015	$0.27	$0.52	$1.07
Internet	PC banking	ATM	telephone	branch

Although the Digital Divide looks likely to exclude players without the requisite level of development, it should be remembered that there have been exclusions before. Large businesses have had shared electronic networks (value-added networks, or VANs) since the 1970s. These were too expensive for smaller players to use or invest in. Now, small businesses and domestic consumers have the opportunity to share in the electronic trend through the Internet. B2B is growing rapidly in terms of volume sales and as a percentage of all e-commerce (see right), but businesses need the communications infrastructure in place and the skilled staff to operate the technology effectively. In 2000 around half of small-to-medium enterprises in the USA were still hesitant about engaging in e-commerce.

US B2B commerce
In 1998 $300 billion, or 3% of GDP, was forecast for 2002; by 2000 the forecast had increased to $843 billion, or 8% of GDP for 2002 .

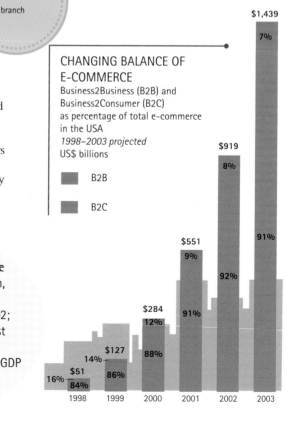

CHANGING BALANCE OF E-COMMERCE
Business2Business (B2B) and Business2Consumer (B2C) as percentage of total e-commerce in the USA
1998–2003 projected
US$ billions

- B2B
- B2C

Year	Total	B2B %	B2C %
1998	$51	84%	16%
1999	$127	86%	14%
2000	$284	88%	12%
2001	$551	91%	9%
2002	$919	92%	8%
2003	$1,439	93%	7%

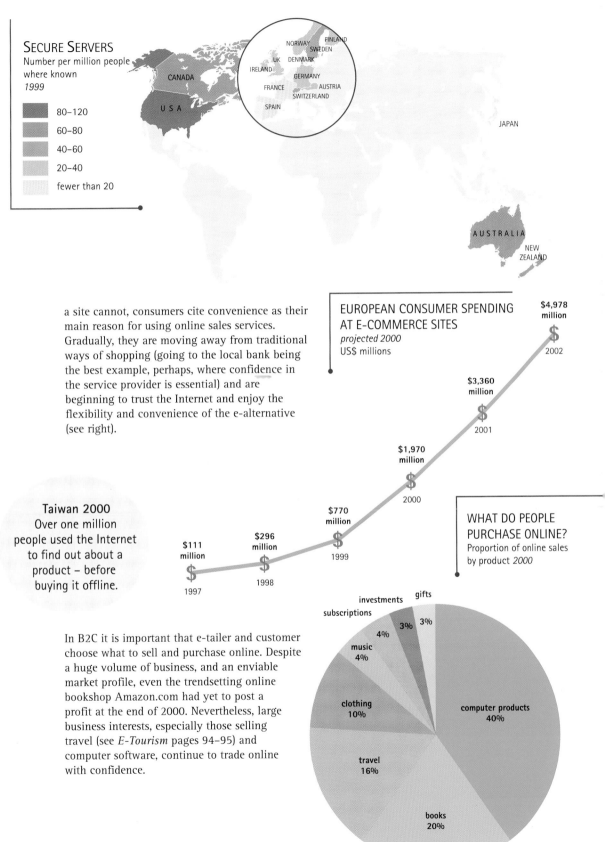

SECURE SERVERS
Number per million people where known
1999

- 80–120
- 60–80
- 40–60
- 20–40
- fewer than 20

CANADA

USA

NORWAY FINLAND
SWEDEN
UK DENMARK
IRELAND
GERMANY
FRANCE AUSTRIA
SWITZERLAND
SPAIN

JAPAN

AUSTRALIA
NEW ZEALAND

a site cannot, consumers cite convenience as their main reason for using online sales services. Gradually, they are moving away from traditional ways of shopping (going to the local bank being the best example, perhaps, where confidence in the service provider is essential) and are beginning to trust the Internet and enjoy the flexibility and convenience of the e-alternative (see right).

EUROPEAN CONSUMER SPENDING AT E-COMMERCE SITES
projected 2000
US$ millions

$4,978 million
$ 2002

$3,360 million
$ 2001

$1,970 million
$ 2000

$770 million
$ 1999

$296 million
$ 1998

$111 million
$ 1997

Taiwan 2000
Over one million people used the Internet to find out about a product – before buying it offline.

WHAT DO PEOPLE PURCHASE ONLINE?
Proportion of online sales by product *2000*

In B2C it is important that e-tailer and customer choose what to sell and purchase online. Despite a huge volume of business, and an enviable market profile, even the trendsetting online bookshop Amazon.com had yet to post a profit at the end of 2000. Nevertheless, large business interests, especially those selling travel (see *E-Tourism* pages 94–95) and computer software, continue to trade online with confidence.

Pie chart:
- computer products 40%
- books 20%
- travel 16%
- clothing 10%
- music 4%
- subscriptions 4%
- investments 3%
- gifts 3%

19

THE PRESS AND RADIO

2

In Malaysia 30% of newspapers are
delivered to the home, 70% are bought
elsewhere. In Norway it is the other way
around: 75% are home deliveries
and 25% are bought on the street.

NEWSPAPER CIRCULATION

High newspaper circulation is often taken as evidence of the openness and vigour of a nation's public deliberation and debate. But as the map shows, high levels of newspaper consumption and freedom of speech do not necessarily go together. Different types of newspaper are used by different people in different ways – for entertainment and information, as well as for keeping up to date with the world of public events – and the way in which newspapers articulate public opinion very much depends on a country's political culture and traditions.

CIRCULATION OF MAJOR NEWSPAPERS WORLDWIDE
Numbers *1995*

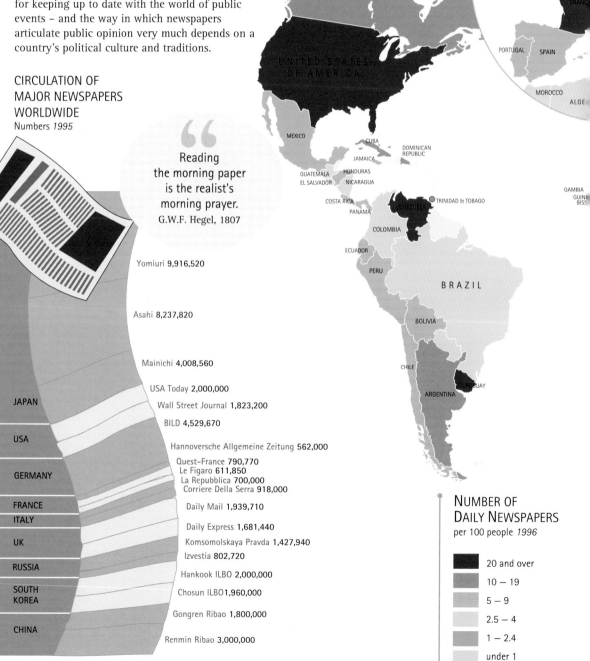

> Reading
> the morning paper
> is the realist's
> morning prayer.
> G.W.F. Hegel, 1807

Yomiuri 9,916,520

Asahi 8,237,820

Mainichi 4,008,560

USA Today 2,000,000

Wall Street Journal 1,823,200

BILD 4,529,670

Hannoversche Allgemeine Zeitung 562,000

Quest–France 790,770
Le Figaro 611,850
La Repubblica 700,000
Corriere Della Serra 918,000

Daily Mail 1,939,710

Daily Express 1,681,440

Komsomolskaya Pravda 1,427,940

Izvestia 802,720

Hankook ILBO 2,000,000

Chosun ILBO 1,960,000

Gongren Ribao 1,800,000

Renmin Ribao 3,000,000

JAPAN

USA

GERMANY

FRANCE
ITALY

UK

RUSSIA

SOUTH KOREA

CHINA

NUMBER OF DAILY NEWSPAPERS
per 100 people *1996*

- 20 and over
- 10 – 19
- 5 – 9
- 2.5 – 4
- 1 – 2.4
- under 1
- other countries

NORWAY
FINLAND
SWEDEN
ESTONIA
LATVIA
LITHUANIA
RMANY
POLAND
BELARUS
CZECH REPUBLIC
SLOVAKIA
UKRAINE
STRIA
HUNGARY
SLOVENIA
CROATIA
YUGOSLAVIA
BULGARIA
ITALY
ALBANIA
MACEDONIA
GREECE

RUSSIA

UKRAINE
KAZAKHSTAN
MONGOLIA
GEORGIA
AZERBAIJAN
UZBEKISTAN
KIRGISTAN
NORTH KOREA
JAPAN
NISIA
TUNISIA
ARMENIA
TAJIKISTAN
SOUTH KOREA
TURKEY
SYRIA
LEBANON
ISRAEL
IRAQ
IRAN
CHINA
JORDAN
KUWA
ALGERIA
LIBYA
EGYPT
SAUDI ARABIA
UAE
PAKISTAN
NEPAL
OMAN
BANGLADESH
Hong Kong
NIGER
CHAD
SUDAN
YEMEN
INDIA
BURMA
LAOS
VIETNAM
BURKINA FASO
THAILAND
TE d'
OIRE
GHANA
TOGO
BENIN
NIGERIA
CENTRAL AFRICAN REPUBLIC
ETHIOPIA
SRI LANKA
PHILIPPINES
CAMEROON
DEMOCRATIC REPUBLIC OF CONGO
UGANDA
GABON
RWANDA
KENYA
MALAYSIA
CONGO
BURUNDI
TANZANIA
INDONESIA
PAPUA NEW GUINEA
ANGOLA
ZAMBIA
ZIMBABWE
NAMIBIA
BOTSWANA
AUSTRALIA
SOUTH AFRICA
NEW ZEALAND

CHANGING CIRCULATIONS
Daily newspapers
per 1,000 inhabitants
1970 and *1997*

    1970
    1997

292
226
107
96
60
29
4.5 8

world
average
developed
countries
developing
countries
least developed
countries

"
Were it left to me to decide
whether we should have
a government without newspapers
or newspapers without government,
I should not hesitate a moment
to prefer the latter.

Thomas Jefferson, 1787

23

Newspapers Online

The growth of the Internet and of online newspapers has led to fears that printed newspapers and magazines will become redundant.

> The year 2000 will signal the end for newspaper and magazine publishers.
>
> Bill Gates
> *World Economic Press,*
> 1998

Undoubtedly, some aspects of the existing press are threatened by the new information and communication technologies. Daily newspapers cannot compete with the Internet for instant delivery of up-to-the-minute news. But people do not read newspapers and magazines solely to gather information. Newspapers deliver a sense of collective, shared identity as well as facts and figures, and it is this aspect that is likely to be more durable. Over the family breakfast table, on the bus or in the subway on the way to work, relaxing in a bar, or waiting in the barber shop, the silent ritual of reading the newspaper is a way of anchoring ourselves in the world of passing events – a way of living in the present – and of establishing a secular communion with our fellow citizens.

The Internet is not the first "new" technology to challenge print. Television has had an effect on newspaper readership, which declined markedly in the USA between 1970 and 1999 (see below). Opinion polls show that people are more likely to trust what they hear on television news than what they read in the papers. But newspapers have survived the advent of both radio and television, and the signs are that they are changing and adapting to face the latest challenge.

The global comparison of newspaper readership illustrated on the previous pages reveals that a flourishing press needs an economy to match. It is no accident that the highest circulation levels are found in the world's wealthiest countries. And although the number of newspapers sold in these countries is decreasing at the same time as Internet usage is increasing, circulation figures there are still far higher than those in the rest of the world.

Established newspapers are rising to the challenge posed by the Internet. Many are setting up their own websites. To some extent, newspapers are driven by a desire always to be first with the news. More importantly, they have woken up to the fact that the storage and retrieval capacity of the Internet potentially makes their archives a new and lucrative source of revenue.

Newspapers are also aware of a threat to the mainstay of their revenue: the humble classified advertisement. The fear is that this income stream could suddenly and decisively be diverted online. Today's press barons want to get in first and control that market too. It is a case of not daring *not* to be there.

However, online newspapers remain loss leaders: while high-profile papers have enjoyed the enhanced international status that an electronic edition brings, many smaller titles are unable to attract the advertising revenue to support their site. Accordingly, the number of sites fluctuates continually (see "Changing Fortunes" opposite).

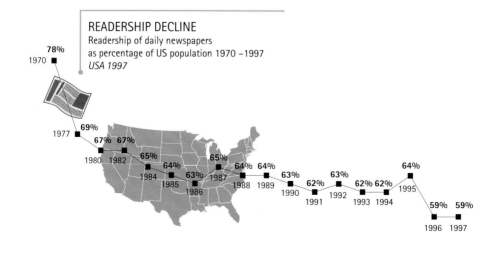

READERSHIP DECLINE
Readership of daily newspapers as percentage of US population 1970 –1997
USA 1997

78% 1970
69% 1977
67% 1980
67% 1982
65% 1984
64% 1985
63% 1986
65% 1987
64% 1988
64% 1989
63% 1990
62% 1991
63% 1992
62% 1993
62% 1994
64% 1995
59% 1996
59% 1997

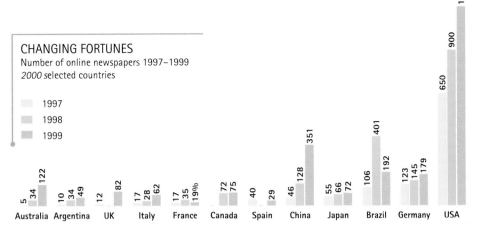

CHANGING FORTUNES
Number of online newspapers 1997–1999
2000 selected countries

- 1997
- 1998
- 1999

	Australia	Argentina	UK	Italy	France	Canada	Spain	China	Japan	Brazil	Germany	USA
1997	5	10		17	17			46	55	106	123	650
1998	34	34	12	28	35	72	40	128	66	401	145	900
1999	122	49	82	62	19%	75	29	351	72	192	179	1,149

If there is a correlation between declining newspaper circulation and the rise of the Internet, it is not in the total number of newspapers in circulation but in the variety of titles available. In developed countries, the number of different titles has declined since the arrival of the Internet. In the USA, for example, the number of daily newspaper titles fell from 1,548 in 1994 to 1,489 in 1998.

People access a wide range of news through the Internet. The key question for the future may be whether the diversity of available media – Internet, print, radio, television – will lead to a similarly diverse range of news and views, or whether the continuing trend towards single ownership across the various media platforms, will limit the editorial range of news and information. The concentration of press ownership inevitably diminishes the claims of the press to articulate the full range of public opinion.

Optimists like to imagine that the press constitutes an independent voice monitoring and chiding the great and the powerful. Whether that role was ever an historical reality rather than a pious hope is doubtful: for example, the two bestselling newspapers in the USA (see page 22), are the *Wall Street Journal*, which deals primarily in financial information, and *USA Today*, which sells tittle-tattle.

CONSUMPTION OF ONLINE NEWS
Percentage of online news users accessing different types of news
USA 2000

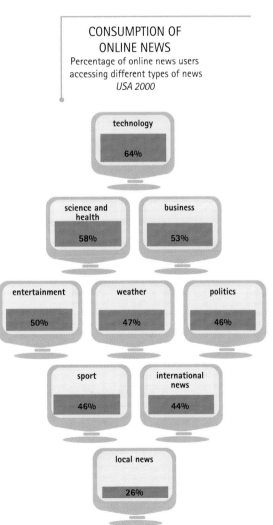

technology 64%

science and health 58%

business 53%

entertainment 50%

weather 47%

politics 46%

sport 46%

international news 44%

local news 26%

LIBERTY OF THE PRESS

The idea of press freedom is more complicated than it first appears. It is a strange kind of right that applies to an institution, the press (that is, newspapers and other news media) and not to individual citizens. And it is a freedom that is not absolute, but one that derives from the social function of the press. If citizens in modern societies are to accept that the decisions and actions of governments are legitimate, they expect those decisions and actions to be subject to public scrutiny. The responsibility of the journalistic media is to provide the forum in which we as citizens can communicate with each other, in a mediated way, about important matters of common concern. To fulfil that responsibility effectively, reporters have to provide reader–citizens with accurate and (reasonably) unbiased information, and journalists must be able to express their opinions freely and without undue external influence. The right of press freedom is necessary for the press to act as a public forum – it is therefore a right the press can claim only if it is carrying out that critical public function.

This is the ideal, of course. The news media have always been about entertainment as much as republican citizenship, and they have all too often been the creatures of megalomaniac proprietors or political interests. Nevertheless, press freedom remains a cornerstone of democracy. That is why it makes the powerful anxious and why journalists are willing to face imprisonment or death in its name (see overleaf).

The degree of press freedom – the number of journalists killed, jailed, attacked and tortured; the number of newspapers banned, confiscated or censored – naturally depends on each country's political situation. Although the situation has generally improved over recent decades (see opposite), especially since the collapse of the Soviet empire in the late 1980s, liberty of the press is unknown to 2.4 billion men and women around the world. For the same number of people it remains random and unreliable. Only 1.2 billion people, or 20 percent of the world's population, can truly be said to enjoy a free press (see below).

Even countries that do enjoy press freedom have their problems. In the USA, where the absence of prior restraint on publication is enshrined in the first amendment to the constitution, there is public cynicism about journalistic irresponsibility. According to research commissioned by anxious newspaper editors, readers are tired of too much sensationalism. They want balanced argument and accurate facts presented fairly. They want the media to explain, regularly, why they act as they do – and why they appear to like stories readers don't like.

At the other end of the spectrum, 1999 was an especially bad year for the number of journalists killed. Estimates range from 34 to 86 – in part depending on whether the Belgrade television

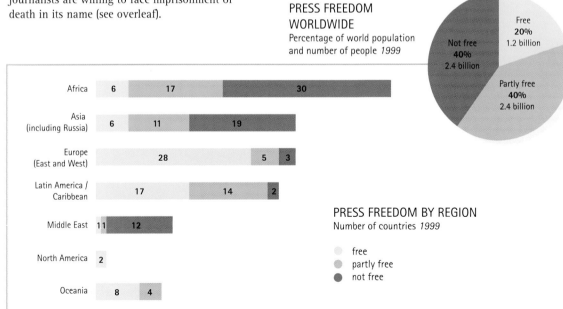

PRESS FREEDOM WORLDWIDE
Percentage of world population and number of people *1999*

Free
20%
1.2 billion

Not free
40%
2.4 billion

Partly free
40%
2.4 billion

PRESS FREEDOM BY REGION
Number of countries *1999*

- free
- partly free
- not free

Africa 6 17 30

Asia (including Russia) 6 11 19

Europe (East and West) 28 5 3

Latin America / Caribbean 17 14 2

Middle East 11 12

North America 2

Oceania 8 4

> There is freedom of
> expression in Iran. But no
> freedom after expression.
>
> Jailed Iranian editor
> Mashallah Shamsolvaezin

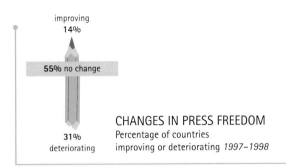

improving
14%

55% no change

31%
deteriorating

CHANGES IN PRESS FREEDOM
Percentage of countries
improving or deteriorating *1997–1998*

workers killed by NATO bombs are included. This peak was out of step with a positive trend in the second half of the 1990s. (During the bleak decade 1985 to 1995, an average of 60 journalists were killed each year.) The worst offender against press freedom was the rebel leader Foday Sankoh in Sierra Leone. His Revolutionary United Front executed at least eight journalists, some with their families, during its bloody occupation of the capital, Freetown in January 1999.

In Burma, in December 1999, 13 journalists were held in prison – most of them connected in some way to Nobel Peace Prize winner Aung San Suu Kyi's opposition National League for Democracy. The Burmese government restricts expression through decrees such as Order 5/96, which prohibits statements that "undermine national stability", backed up by zealous censors and by security services happy to resort to intimidation, threats and torture. Foreign journalists are generally denied visas to travel to Burma and at least five reporters using tourist visas were deported during 1999. Fax machines, photocopiers and computer modems are illegal, there are no independent newspapers, and foreign broadcasts are frequently jammed.

In Iran, press freedom suffers in the power struggle between the reformist president Mohammad Khatami and the hard-line supreme leader, Ayatollah Ali Khamenei. In April 2000, Khamenei thundered against a conspiracy of "10 to 15 newspapers. . .whose only aim is to create tension and make people cynical of the regime". In less than a week, Iran's judiciary had banned 16 publications, decimating the burgeoning pro-reform press.

Although there are equally grim tales to tell about Angola, China, Cuba, Tunisia, Kazakhstan, Turkey and other blackspots, and growing worries about places such as Russia, Sri Lanka and Venezuela,

there are also signs of hope. Under President Wahid, Indonesia has introduced a commission to protect press freedom. In May 2000, the New York-based Committee to Protect Journalists named ten leading enemies of press freedom. Among them were Slobodan Milosevic of Yugoslavia and Alberto Fujimori of Peru. By the end of 2000, both had been thrown out of office.

Over 50% of readers
questioned in the USA in 1999
believed the press had too much
freedom, up from 38% in 1997;
only 63% believed newspapers
should be able to publish freely
without government approval,
down from 80%.

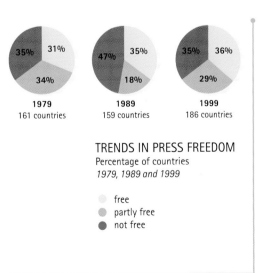

1979	1989	1999
161 countries	159 countries	186 countries

1979: 35%, 31%, 34%
1989: 47%, 35%, 18%
1999: 35%, 36%, 29%

TRENDS IN PRESS FREEDOM
Percentage of countries
1979, 1989 and 1999

○ free
◐ partly free
● not free

This map, and the charts on the previous pages, are based on the ratings system devised by the US-based Freedom House. The organization looks at both the print media and the broadcast media, assesses the laws and administrative decisions that affect the content of news media, evaluates the degree of political influence or control over the content of news and examines the economic influences on news content, whether from governments, corporations or other interests. Finally, it records actual violations against the media, including murder, physical attacks, harassment and censorship.

In some places, the judgment of Freedom House may appear a little ideological to non-American eyes. Their scepticism towards public service broadcasting seems surprising to observers familiar with European, Canadian and Australian models. In these societies, many people still see public service as a counter to the trend towards monopolies and cartels in unregulated media markets. They view it as a guarantee that diverse voices will be heard and as an effective structural defence of public interest as well as private profit in the regulation of the news media. The findings of Freedom House have therefore been cross-checked against those of the French-based Reporters Sans Frontières. The two are very close to one another.

NUMBER OF JOURNALISTS IMPRISONED
At year end 1997–2000

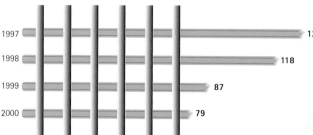

Year	Number
1997	129
1998	118
1999	87
2000	79

> The time, it is to be hoped,
> is gone by when the defense would be
> necessary of the "liberty of the press"
> as one of the securities against
> corrupt or tyrannical government.
> John Stuart Mill, *On Liberty*, 1859

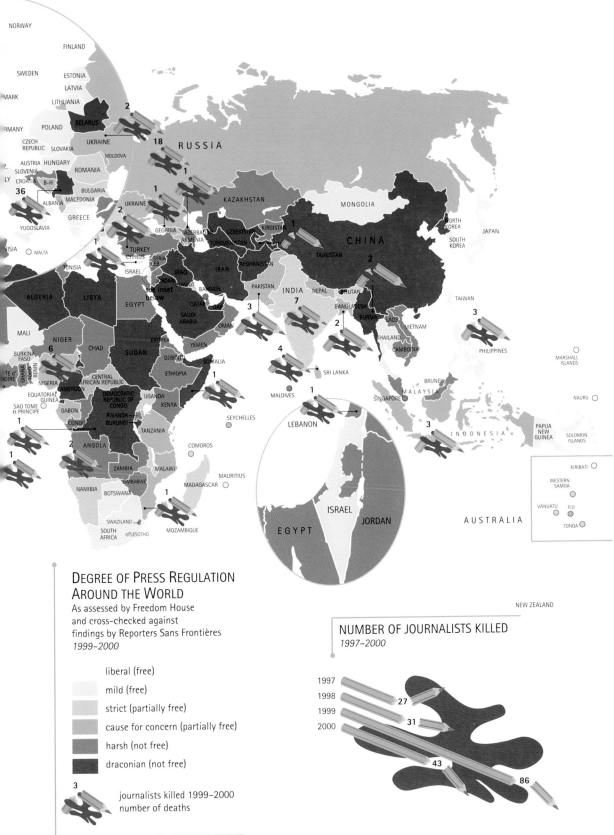

DEGREE OF PRESS REGULATION AROUND THE WORLD
As assessed by Freedom House
and cross-checked against
findings by Reporters Sans Frontières
1999–2000

liberal (free)

mild (free)

strict (partially free)

cause for concern (partially free)

harsh (not free)

draconian (not free)

3
journalists killed 1999–2000
number of deaths

NUMBER OF JOURNALISTS KILLED
1997–2000

1997	27
1998	31
1999	43
2000	86

NEW ZEALAND

29

RADIO

Although radio is one of the oldest forms of mass media, at the beginning of the 21st century it is also one of the most vibrant. Its popularity is widespread – with rich and poor, and with those globally networked and those most isolated. While many developing nations rely on radio for their access to world news and local information networks, there are also many developed economies that listen to digital radio, that is, radio delivered via the Web. More advanced still are those radio producers experimenting with radio that is not just broadcast online, but also produced online in a virtual environment. This allows radio stations to use images as well as sound ("streaming"), and to find a market niche – rather the same struggle as that of the print media as they go online.

When Marconi invented wireless technology at the very end of the 19th century he thought he had created a system of personal communication. However, the telephone, patented in 1876, had already cornered the domestic communications market, and wireless technology was used in the management of warfare, colonization and intelligence gathering. It was also developed, not as a means of one-to-one communication, but of broadcasting to whole nations.

The first national broadcasting companies (the NBC in the USA, and the BBC in the UK) took their public responsiblity very seriously. In 1922 Marconi, which spearheaded wireless technology and commercialization in the USA, realized that public service was a mainstay of NBC's role in the US media landscape. The radio or "wireless" set was a tool of education, entertainment and national consciousness raising. Radio programmers assumed responsibility for the moral health of the nation. This view soon changed in the USA, where the possibility of taking adverts straight into the living room or kitchen was too tempting to resist. In the UK there was a more avuncular, or patronising, attitude to the public, and commercial radio was kept at bay by the BBC's 1925 anti-marketing remit.

Radio content continues to provide interesting snapshots of national and global tastes, priorities and audio habits. In the USA, radio stations typically broadcast religion, classic rock, and news. In 2000 the BBC announced that Children's Hour – one of the original staples of public broadcasting in the UK – would return to Radio 4 for a trial one-year run.

ONLINE RADIO IN USA
Number of online stations
in selected states *2000*

9 North Dakota
31 Maryland
93 Washington
100 Florida
177 California
180 Texas

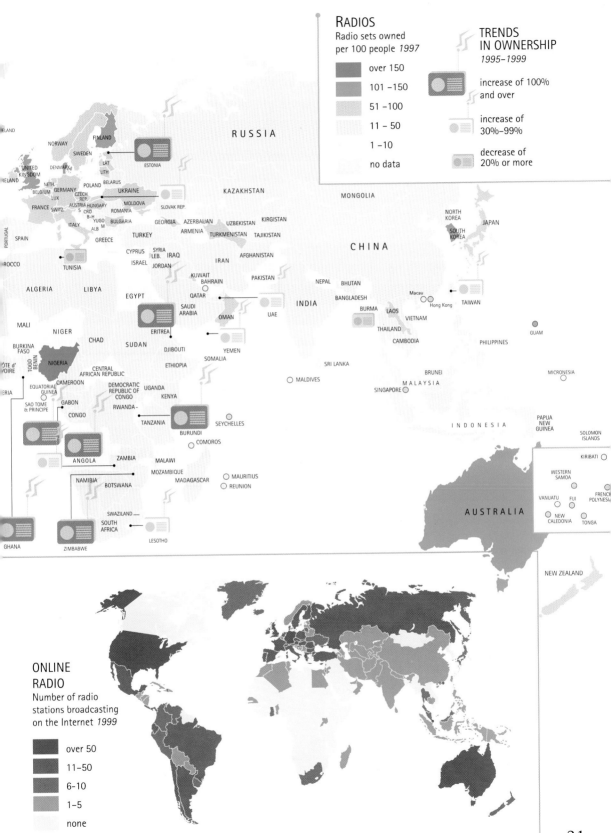

RADIOS
Radio sets owned per 100 people *1997*
- over 150
- 101–150
- 51–100
- 11–50
- 1–10
- no data

TRENDS IN OWNERSHIP *1995–1999*
- increase of 100% and over
- increase of 30%–99%
- decrease of 20% or more

ONLINE RADIO
Number of radio stations broadcasting on the Internet *1999*
- over 50
- 11–50
- 6–10
- 1–5
- none

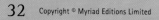

CINEMA

Animation is a growing feature in cinematic production, aided by the possibilities of digital effects. In the USA gross takings on animated releases jumped from $187.3 million in 1997 to $611.4 million in 1999.

THE FALL AND RISE OF THE BIG SCREEN

Although audiences still go to the movies in their millions, they now also watch films on free-to-air, satellite and cable television, on copied, rented or purchased videos and DVDs – legitimate or pirated – and, in some places, through video-on-demand down a telephone line. The integrated industry of movie production, distribution and exhibition is a thing of the past. Old technologies, old ways of doing things and old institutional boundaries have gone. In another sense, though, cinema remains as far ahead of the game as it has always been.

Early movie pioneers quickly spotted the potential for globalization, and developed the organizational structures and marketing techniques to capitalize on it. By the 1920s, thanks in part to the devastation of European cinema by World War I, US companies were setting up a worldwide network of partnerships and franchises through which to control international distribution. The chaos of European cinema after World War II in the 1940s consolidated Hollywood's global dominance – a position it has never lost.

The fascination of cinema lies in the magic of making distant worlds present, or of conjuring up compelling fictional worlds. The next spread shows how Hollywood has been able to package that power. This spread demonstrates that the key to revenue in the film business remains distribution and exhibition. Audiences rent from exhibitors a couple of hours in which they can be moved, uplifted or simply distracted. Exhibitors rent from distributors the right to exploit their intellectual property.

Today, the leading Hollywood distributors – Buena Vista, Columbia, Fox, UIP, Universal and Warner Bros – take 83 percent of the market in Latin America and 70 percent of the revenue in Europe. In 1999 only two of the UK's top ten films were released by independent producers. One was *Notting Hill*, the year's second most successful film, released by PolyGram; the other, *Austin Powers: The Spy Who Shagged Me*, was released by Entertainment. By the end of the year, PolyGram had been swallowed up by Universal.

TRENDS IN
BOX OFFICE
REVENUE
1996 to 1999
2000

1996-97
1997-98
1998-99

In the rest of the world, only the massive Indian market has resisted Hollywood's siren call, with the US industry cornering no more than 4 percent of the market. The USA remains the world's largest single market by a huge margin, however. In 1998 the revenue earned there increased to over 40 percent of the world total.

GROSS BOX OFFICE REVENUE
2000 or latest available data
US$

$5 billion or more	$100 million – $300 million
$1 billion – $5 billion	$10 million – $100 million
$500 million – $1 billion	less than $10 million
$300 million – $500 million	no data

+21% **+12%** **+7%** **-3%**

NORWAY
FINLAND
SWEDEN
ESTONIA
LATVIA
DENMARK
LITHUANIA
GERMANY POLAND
CZECH REPUBLIC SLOVAKIA
AUSTRIA HUNGARY
SWITZ. SLOVENIA ROMANIA
CROATIA
ITALY YUGOSLAVIA BULGARIA
GREECE

POLAND

RUSSIA

CHINA **+4%** **-8%**
SOUTH KOREA
JAPAN **+7% +7%**
TAIWAN
Hong Kong

TURKEY
CYPRUS
ISRAEL
KUWAIT
EGYPT
PAKISTAN
INDIA **+17%** **+4%**

THAILAND
PHILIPPINES

KENYA

MALAYSIA
SINGAPORE

INDONESIA

AUSTRALIA **+3%** **-9%**

NEW ZEALAND

Europe inset
ICELAND
NORWAY
FINLAND
SWEDEN
ESTONIA
UNITED KINGDOM
DENMARK
LATVIA
LITHUANIA
IRELAND
NETH.
BELGIUM
LUX.
GERMANY POLAND
CZ. REP
SLOVAKIA
FRANCE
AUSTRIA HUNG.
SWITZ. SLO.
CRO.
ROMANIA
ITALY YUG. BULGARIA
PORTUGAL SPAIN
GREECE
MOROCCO

CANADA
UNITED STATES OF AMERICA
MEXICO

SOUTH AFRICA

TURKEY
CYPRUS
ISRAEL
EGYPT
CHINA
PAKISTAN
INDIA
TAIWAN
Hong Kong
THAILAND
PHILIPPINES
SOUTH KOREA
JAPAN

PANAMA
VENEZUELA
COLOMBIA
ECUADOR
PERU
BRAZIL
BOLIVIA
PARAGUAY
CHILE
URUGUAY
ARGENTINA

KENYA
SOUTH AFRICA

MALAYSIA
SINGAPORE
INDONESIA
AUSTRALIA
NEW ZEALAND

TICKET PRICES
US$ *1998*

$10.00 and over	
$5.00 – $9.99	
$1.00 – $4.99	
less than $1.00	
no data	

HOLLYWOOD

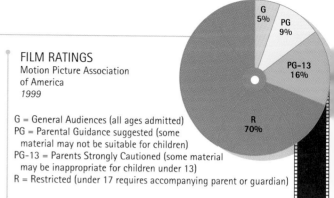

In the 1940s, the anthropologist Hortense Powdermaker, astutely called Hollywood a "dream factory". Between 1915 and 1917, some 20 years after the invention of the technology, the "killer application" had been established: the creation and dissemination of stories told through moving pictures. These fictions or fantasies played endless variations on a few basic narrative structures, and they were peopled by glamorous figures, both like us and yet wholly unattainable. The formula captured audiences' imaginations around the world. And these dreams were manufactured in the factories of Hollywood.

By the 1930s, the Hollywood studio system was firmly in place. Dominated by the five major studios – MGM, Paramount, Twentieth Century Fox, Universal and Warner Brothers – Hollywood effectively became a cartel that controlled all aspects of production, distribution and exhibition. The studios applied the same principles of mass production and time-and-motion efficiency to the film business as the Ford Motor Company did to producing cars. They employed scriptwriters, directors, carpenters and publicists. They made the stars. Meticulous project management meant that a dozen or more films could be in production at the same time, making sure all the studio's resources were being used to maximum efficiency. Even so, and although making movies may be the glamorous part of the business, production has always been a high-risk *cost* that is only recouped as films are distributed and exhibited.

After World War II the major studios were forced into a radical reorganization by two events. One was the US Supreme Court's judgment in the so-called "Paramount case" in the 1940s. An anti-trust suit had been brought against the five fully integrated majors and three other distributors. It was found that their vertical integration – that is, the way they controlled all aspects of cinema – enabled them to operate in non-competitive ways. As a result, the studios were required to divorce their production and distribution activities from exhibition. As if this were not bad enough, in the early 1950s the studios had to face the advent of television and a subsequent collapse in cinema attendance (see *The Moviegoers* pages 42–43). Between 1946 and 1956 box office receipts in the USA fell by 40 percent, and cinema audiences halved.

FILM RATINGS
Motion Picture Association
of America
1999

G = General Audiences (all ages admitted)
PG = Parental Guidance suggested (some material may not be suitable for children)
PG-13 = Parents Strongly Cautioned (some material may be inappropriate for children under 13)
R = Restricted (under 17 requires accompanying parent or guardian)

Although some studios were slow to react, and some may have underestimated the power of television, forward-looking film executives had been involved in experiments with television technologies from the 1920s onwards. Even as they began to be taken over by larger conglomerates, the major studios began to see television not just as a threat, but as a potential outlet. They moved into television production and they bought television networks. They moved away from mass film production. They began to shed their huge workforces. They sold off the physical sites associated with the factory system, or else turned them into Hollywood theme parks. They created a new way of doing business, and helped to pioneer the new "weightless" economy.

At the begining of the 21st century Warners, Fox, Walt Disney, Columbia and Universal act primarily as investors rather than as producers, allowing independent companies to put together production

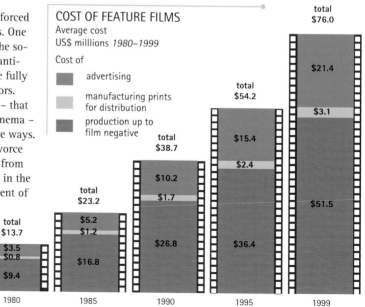

COST OF FEATURE FILMS
Average cost
US$ milllions *1980–1999*

Cost of
- advertising
- manufacturing prints for distribution
- production up to film negative

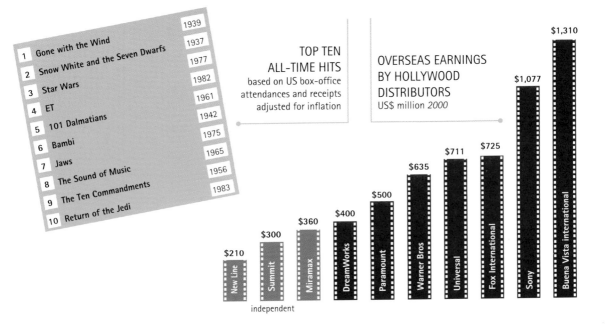

	TOP TEN ALL-TIME HITS based on US box-office attendances and receipts adjusted for inflation
1	Gone with the Wind — 1939
2	Snow White and the Seven Dwarfs — 1937
3	Star Wars — 1977
4	ET — 1982
5	101 Dalmatians — 1961
6	Bambi — 1942
7	Jaws — 1975
8	The Sound of Music — 1965
9	The Ten Commandments — 1956
10	Return of the Jedi — 1983

OVERSEAS EARNINGS BY HOLLYWOOD DISTRIBUTORS
US$ million *2000*

New Line $210 (independent)
Summit $300
Miramax $360
DreamWorks $400
Paramount $500
Warner Bros $635
Universal $711
Fox International $725
Sony $1,077
Buena Vista international $1,310

packages and to assemble production teams – and also to take most of the financial risk.

Production costs continue to rise (see below left), with averages boosted by the huge expense of blockbusters such as *Titanic* and *The Phantom Menace*. Hollywood is an economy of hits and flops. A dud might destroy a production company. Distributors hedge against disaster by lavishing huge advertising budgets on their products, and relying on the one-in-ten chance of a smash hit to offset the losers. Of the films made in the USA and presented to the Motion Picture Association for rating in 1999, only around 75 percent were distributed for exhibition in movie theaters. Some disappear without trace, others are released directly into the video market.

Although the major studios were happy enough to shed the burden of production, they cling ferociously to their control of the distribution of both domestic and international films, not only in the USA, but around the world (see "Overseas Earnings" above). The top five or six companies routinely collect almost 90 percent of US theatrical film rentals. Since the 1980s, they have replicated this stranglehold in relation to video, satellite and cable. Hollywood movies probably account for about 90 percent of video rentals and 60 percent of video purchases – a market that is growing rapidly (see right). Indeed, video sales can produce a greater revenue than theater exhibition: the Disney film *Tarzan* grossed US$171 million in box-office receipts in 1999, but US$268 million from its video release in 2000.

The major studios' position of strength provides them with the funds to invest in production. This gives them the economic muscle to impose their terms on the independent producers, who are almost entirely dependent on the studios for distributing and marketing their products. The 1990s were good years for the new lean, mean and network-based Hollywood. Box-office revenues in the USA revived (see *The Fall and Rise of the Big Screen*, pages 34–35), and the majors maintained their position as providers of television content worldwide. In the 21st century – the second century of cinema – Hollywood will no doubt seize the opportunities offered by emerging new media and continue to fascinate the world with its immaterial commodities, its dreams.

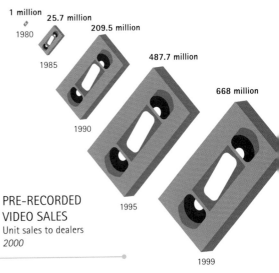

1 million — 1980
25.7 million — 1985
209.5 million — 1990
487.7 million — 1995
668 million — 1999

PRE-RECORDED VIDEO SALES
Unit sales to dealers *2000*

FORTRESS EUROPE?

European audiences have always loved Hollywood films. Even so, the 20th century witnessed an undeclared, non-violent but hard-fought European war against the USA – or, specifically, against Hollywood. In the 1920s, the inroads made by US entertainment, leisure and advertising industries prompted warnings from across the European political spectrum against the "Hollywood octopus" and its dire cultural consequences. A war of words has continued ever since. European governments have, at different times, attempted to regulate the economic and cultural impact of US films by imposing quotas on their importation or by subsidising and promoting domestic film production. For all their anti-protectionist rhetoric, the US film industry and its international lobby organization, the Motion Picture Association (MPA), have fiercely protected the interests of a small group of US companies by deploying State Department officials and, not infrequently, US presidents to put pressure on any nation daring to mess with the divine right of US capitalism to sell its goods unhindered around the globe.

The Euro-Hollywood war hotted up in 1993 as the establishment of the European Union (EU) created an enticing single market of 336 million consumers. Even though the EU's economic commissioners may sympathize with the MPA's liberalizing instincts, its cultural commissioners remain passionate about preserving cultural diversity and national identities. The old conflicts flared bitterly in the lead-up to the 1994 General Agreement on Tariffs and Trade (GATT). The Europeans, led by the French, took negotiations to the wire by insisting that cinema and television should be treated primarily as cultural issues, and not just as another industry. US negotiators expressed – no doubt strategic – outrage and incomprehension at the very idea that Hollywood's worldwide domination might have cultural implications. For them, this was purely business.

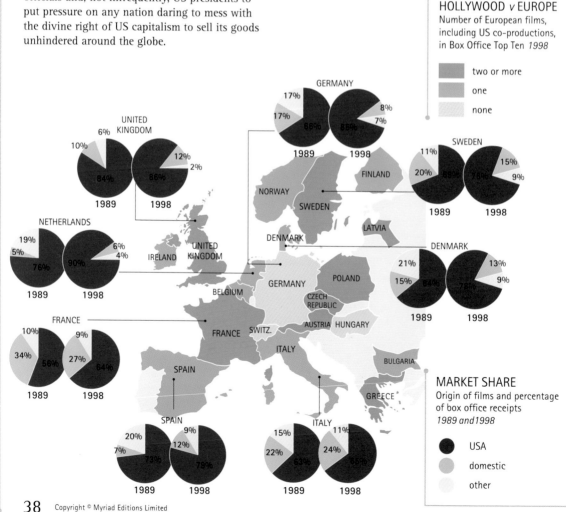

TOP TEN:
HOLLYWOOD v EUROPE
Number of European films, including US co-productions, in Box Office Top Ten *1998*

- two or more
- one
- none

MARKET SHARE
Origin of films and percentage of box office receipts
1989 and 1998

- USA
- domestic
- other

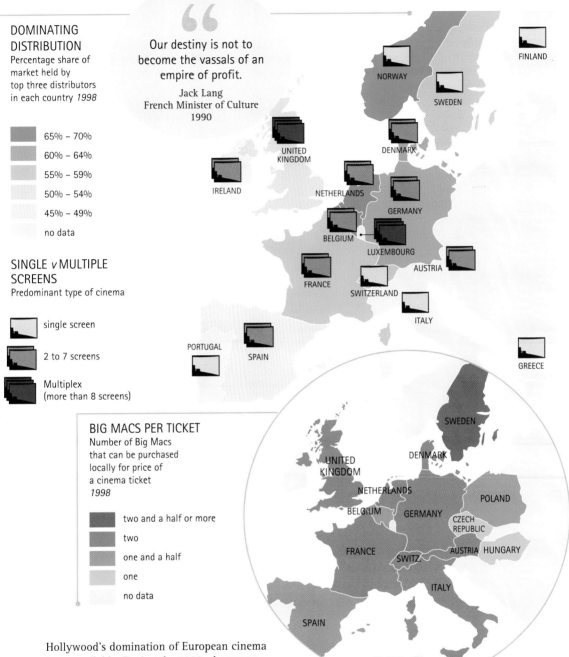

DOMINATING DISTRIBUTION

Percentage share of market held by top three distributors in each country *1998*

- 65% – 70%
- 60% – 64%
- 55% – 59%
- 50% – 54%
- 45% – 49%
- no data

SINGLE *v* MULTIPLE SCREENS

Predominant type of cinema

- single screen
- 2 to 7 screens
- Multiplex (more than 8 screens)

BIG MACS PER TICKET

Number of Big Macs that can be purchased locally for price of a cinema ticket *1998*

- two and a half or more
- two
- one and a half
- one
- no data

> **Our destiny is not to become the vassals of an empire of profit.**
>
> Jack Lang
> French Minister of Culture
> 1990

NORWAY
FINLAND
SWEDEN
DENMARK
UNITED KINGDOM
IRELAND
NETHERLANDS
GERMANY
BELGIUM
LUXEMBOURG
AUSTRIA
FRANCE
SWITZERLAND
ITALY
PORTUGAL
SPAIN
GREECE

SWEDEN
DENMARK
UNITED KINGDOM
NETHERLANDS
POLAND
BELGIUM
GERMANY
CZECH REPUBLIC
FRANCE
SWITZ.
AUSTRIA
HUNGARY
ITALY
SPAIN

Hollywood's domination of European cinema is unassailable. During the 1990s, however, Europeans started to go to the movies more often, and enjoyed a significant growth in the number and quality of screens, especially in multiplexes (see above). Production in EU countries also increased – by over 10 percent in 1999 alone.

In the end, this particular cold war works reasonably well for both sides. Hollywood takes 70 percent of the revenue from cinemas in Europe.

Audiences across the continent are able to enjoy Hollywood's genius for popular entertainment. At the same time, interventionist policies allow national, and sometimes minority, audiences the chance of seeing other, indigenous types of film that would otherwise be denied them.

THE SILVER SCREEN

In Hollywood's heyday, the major studios controlled the exhibition, or screening of movies, as well as all other aspects of cinema. They owned key downtown first-run movie theaters, and ensured that likely hit movies were released in their theaters before being shown elsewhere. They made sure that second- or third-string chains could not pick and choose from their output, but had to show run-of-the-mill offerings as well as the season's winners. In the 1950s, the major studios were forced out of the business of exhibiting movies by the US Supreme Court's decision in the Paramount case (see *Hollywood* pages 36-37). Since then, exhibitors have had to respond to the availability of films on video, satellite and cable television, and other outlets. Increasingly, the pressure is to recoup investment as quickly as possible.

The radical break came with the release of Steven Spielberg's *Jaws* in 1975. Previously a blanket release in hundreds of theaters had been reserved for sure-fire flops. Universal realized that television might be an effective marketing tool – until then it had scarcely been used to advertise films. The studio spent an unprecedented US$700,000 on 30-second prime-time slots as *Jaws* was released in 409 cinemas. The rest is history. Today a blockbuster, such as *Gladiator*, may be released on more than 2,000 screens across the USA and, with saturation television advertising, generate its highest receipts in the first week of opening.

Screen-hungry blanket releases have been one factor fuelling the growth in multiplexes, at least in economically-advanced countries. Other factors include the re-entry of the major distributors into exhibition in the deregulated 1980s, and the cinema-owners' need to provide a better experience in terms of surroundings, facilities and projection quality if they are to compete with home-based movie-watching. Despite these developments, changing stock market fashions have hit US exhibition. The leading circuits, United Artists, Carmike General Cinemas and Edwards, all filed for bankruptcy in 2000, with giants Regal and Loews teetering on the brink.

Electronic cinema is being touted as the next big thing in exhibition. Finally doing away with the need for those clumsy reels of film, e-cinema allows a "film" to be stored digitally as a data file and then transmitted by satellite, DVD or cable to movie theaters, which screen it using high-definition electronic projectors. This technique was pioneered for high-profile sporting events and used experimentally in 1999 to screen George Lucas's *The Phantom Menace*. It is predicted that there will be 10,000 digital screens worldwide by 2005, with all exhibition going digital within 20 years. The new technology is expected to slash print production and distribution costs – currently worth nearly US$5 billion globally – by over 90 percent and change, yet again, the way the cinema industry does its business.

SCREEN DENSITY
Number of screens per million people
2000 or latest available data

- over 100 screens
- 75 – 100 screens
- 50 – 74 screens
- 25 – 49 screens
- fewer than 25
- no data

NORWAY
FINLAND
SWEDEN
ESTONIA
LATVIA
MARK
LITHUANIA
RMANY
POLAND
CZECH REPUBLIC
SLOVAKIA
AUSTRIA HUNGARY
SLOVENIA
ROMANIA
CROATIA
YUGOSLAVIA
ITALY
BULGARIA
GREECE

RUSSIA

KAZAKHSTAN

GEORGIA
AZERBAIJAN
TAJIKISTAN
TURKEY
CYPRUS
ISRAEL
SYRIA
LEB
JORDAN
IRAN
CHINA
KUWAIT
BAHRAIN
QATAR
UAE
PAKISTAN
EGYPT
OMAN
INDIA
YEMEN

SOUTH KOREA
JAPAN

TAIWAN
BURMA
LAOS
Hong Kong
VIETNAM
THAILAND

PHILIPPINES

TE d'IOIRE
BENIN
CAMEROON
ETHIOPIA
KENYA
RWANDA
TANZANIA

SRI LANKA

MALAYSIA
SINGAPORE
INDONESIA

ZIMBABWE
MADAGASCAR
MAURITIUS

SOUTH AFRICA

AUSTRALIA

NEW ZEALAND

RELEASE OF *GLADIATOR* IN THE USA
Number of screens and box office takings
2000

Box office takings per week US$		Number of screens on which film was showing
$2.6m	week ending July 16, 2000	1,034
$4.2m	week ending July 9, 2000	1,210
$4.3m	week ending July 4, 2000	1,411
$6.4m	week ending June 25, 2000	1,812
$8.8m	week ending June 18, 2000	2,266
$11.2m	week ending June 11, 2000	2,706
$11.9m	week ending June 4, 2000	3,056
$24.0m	week ending May 28, 2000	3,188
$29.5m	week ending May 21, 2000	3,041
$38.8m	week ending May 14, 2000	2,943
$34.8m	weekend May 5–7, 2000	2,938

41

THE MOVIEGOERS

In cultural terms, cinema – and especially Hollywood cinema – was the defining medium of the 20th century. Cinema taught impressionable young men and women how to dress, how to kiss, how to desire, how to dream. Its images and sounds haunted their minds. To look at the long history of cinema attendance in the UK from 1933 to 1999 is to see not just industry statistics, but also a social and cultural history (see "Cinema admissions in the UK" opposite). A weekly visit to the movies became a national habit during World War II, until the arrival of television provoked a shift away from the public space of the cinema to the defensive home as the place where families enjoyed their audio-visual entertainment. A long, depressing slump followed from the 1950s until the 1980s, as film-makers, distributors and exhibitors struggled to come to terms with the loss of the mass audience. Then, from the trough of the mid-1980s, there was a gradual and paradoxical revival of movie-going – paradoxical because it coincided with the home-video revolution, which consolidated the domestication of leisure but at the same time seems to have whetted audiences' appetite for the "real thing" – the big screen experience.

The revival in attendance in the 1990s was neither global nor consistent (see "Trends in cinema attendance by region"). Overall, there was a massive decline in the size of the cinema audience around the world in the last decade or so of the 20th century. The audience in India halved (but still remain far and away the world's largest); in China movie-going collapsed from nearly 19 *billion* visits in 1988 to just 121 *million* a decade later (due in part to the availability of cheap compact video disk players and pirated films on disk). The cinema revival has been limited to the affluent regions of North America, Western Europe, and Australasia. Because of the *Titanic* phenomenon, 1998 was an exceptionally good year – except in the UK, for some reason, which saw a dip. In the USA, there was a slight post-*Titanic* decrease in admissions in 1999, but ticket sales were still 80 million ahead of 1997.

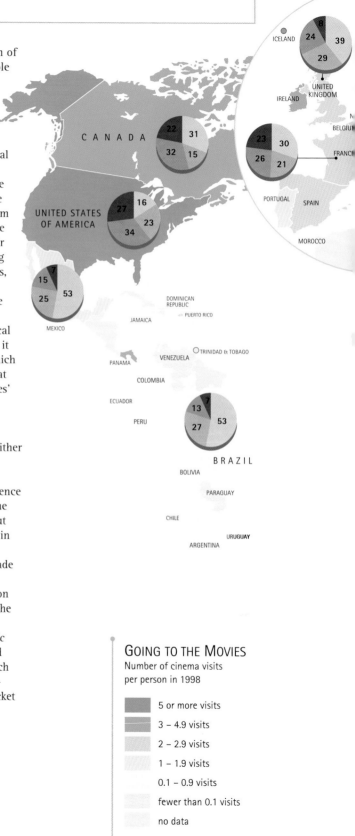

GOING TO THE MOVIES
Number of cinema visits per person in 1998

- 5 or more visits
- 3 – 4.9 visits
- 2 – 2.9 visits
- 1 – 1.9 visits
- 0.1 – 0.9 visits
- fewer than 0.1 visits
- no data

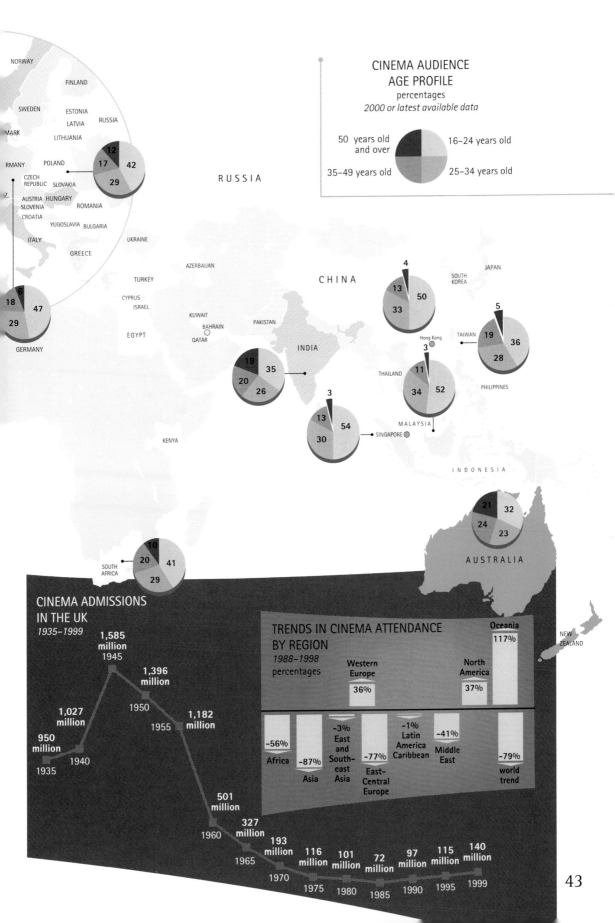

CINEMA AUDIENCE
AGE PROFILE
percentages
2000 or latest available data

50 years old and over | 16–24 years old
35–49 years old | 25–34 years old

CINEMA ADMISSIONS IN THE UK
1935–1999

1,585 million 1945
1,396 million 1950
1,027 million
1,182 million 1955
950 million
1940
1935
501 million
327 million 1960
193 million 1965
116 million 1970
101 million 1975
72 million 1980
97 million 1985
115 million 1990
140 million 1995
1999

TRENDS IN CINEMA ATTENDANCE BY REGION
1988–1998 percentages

Oceania 117%
Western Europe 36%
North America 37%

Africa −56%
Asia −87%
East and South-east Asia −3%
East-Central Europe −77%
Latin America Caribbean −1%
Middle East −41%
world trend −79%

43

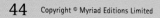

TELEVISION AND BEYOND

Between 1996 and 1999 broadcast television's
share of total media consumption in the USA
fell from 59% to 45%. Over the same period,
cable and satellite television's share rose
from 35% to 45%.

4

TELEVISION WORLDWIDE

Television was available as early as 1936, although television sets were not mass-produced until the late 1940s, after World War II. Since then television has grown into one of the most powerful media the world has known. It provides both entertainment and education, can be used as an effective vehicle for propaganda, and has helped to forge national identities in countries around the world.

Although television has reached over 90 percent of people in all developed countries, and over 80 percent even in many developing countries, including China, people do not all have their own set, nor do they watch television in the same manner. In the more industrialized countries, many young people have a television in their own room (see opposite). Those with access to television in rural Africa and Asia, however, often watch it in public venues, or as part of a large family group. Although access to radio is reasonably widespread in Africa (see *Radio* pages 30–31), access to television is not. While 60 percent of Africans live in areas covered by radio networks, television coverage tends to be confined to those living in medium or large towns. Unesco estimates that only 3.5 percent of those living in Sub-Saharan Africa own a set, compared with a world average of 23 percent.

In countries whose populations comprise different ethnic groups there are huge potential markets and possibilities for television services. In India, for example, Hindi, the majority language, is spoken as a first language by 337 million people, but at least 15 "minority" languages are also used, including Bengali, with 70 million speakers, and Tamil, with 53 million. Clearly, there is a vast market for "local" networks. Although almost 70 million homes, amounting to 362 million domestic viewers, in India have a television, there are 70 million without. Most users access programs via satellite or cable – an estimated 30 million homes have cable TV – but only one home in 20 has relatively trouble-free transmission. This is blamed on the unwillingness of cable providers to deal with Indian government regulations and quality requirements, which is an issue that all television service providers will have to face.

In China television has only reached a large audience since the mid-1980s. Minority groups and language differences are currently served largely by cable services, which are rapidly increasing their coverage. More rural Chinese have access to cable TV than to fixed telephones.

IRELAND · UNITED KINGDOM

BELG

PORT

DOMINICAN REPUBLIC

PUERTO RICO

GUATEMALA

COSTA RICA · TRINIDAD & TOBAGO

PANAMA · VENEZUELA

COLOMBIA

ECUADOR

BRAZIL

CHILE

URUGUAY

ARGENTINA

ACCESS TO CABLE TV IN CHINA
1989–1999
millions

1989 — 11.1
1990 — 13
1991 — 16.5
1992 — 21
1993 — 28
1994 — 36
1995 — 45
1996 — 53.2
1997 — 63
1998 — 71.9
1999 — 80

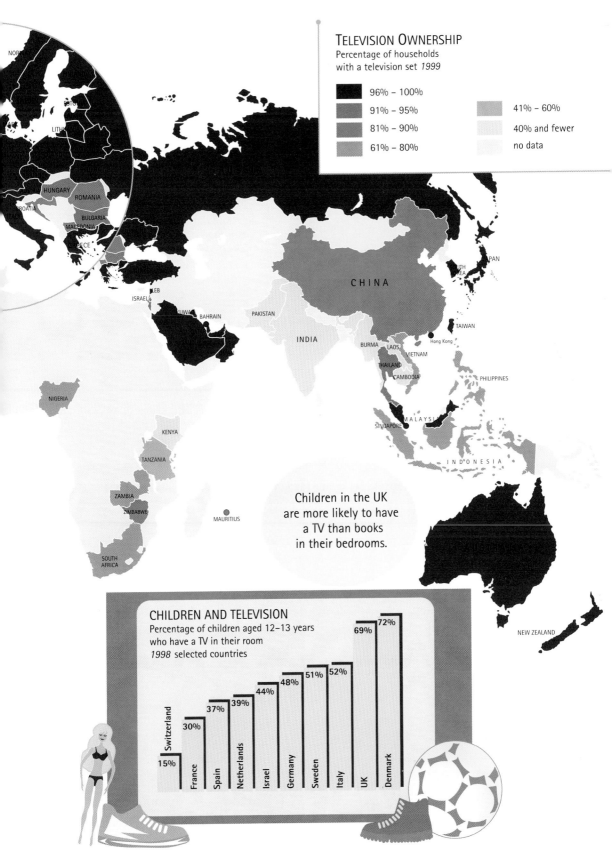

TELEVISION OWNERSHIP
Percentage of households
with a television set *1999*

- 96% – 100%
- 91% – 95%
- 81% – 90%
- 61% – 80%
- 41% – 60%
- 40% and fewer
- no data

Children in the UK
are more likely to have
a TV than books
in their bedrooms.

CHILDREN AND TELEVISION
Percentage of children aged 12–13 years
who have a TV in their room
1998 selected countries

Country	Percentage
Switzerland	15%
France	30%
Spain	37%
Netherlands	39%
Israel	44%
Germany	48%
Sweden	51%
Italy	52%
UK	69%
Denmark	72%

LOCAL *v* GLOBAL, PUBLIC *v* COMMERCIAL

The beginning of the 21st century is a phase of great commercial diversity. The development of digital TV is causing heightened levels of competition between content providers, and providing both threats and opportunities in those countries where public-service broadcasting still exists. The new technology is often the scapegoat for the way in which technology is deployed, the content it is used to disseminate, and the patterns of ownership that underpin its development. But digital TV does not necessarily mean deregulation, or loss of public-service channels. Neither does it have to be global. It could cater for local audiences, and even for smaller interest groups. The technology clearly provides enormous scope for networks and content providers, who need to be imaginative and creative about how they use it.

There is concern that the non-commercial options open to public-service broadcasters are under attack. This is blamed on the deregulation of the market place, which brings with it an over-emphasis on competition. Quality programs, it is argued, are affordable only with the help of government subsidy and public-license payments. It is anecdotally true that a certain kind of quality, and especially programming relevant to local audiences, has been associated with public service and subsidy. One could also argue, however, that commercial providers and government regulators could work together with the public-service networks to produce a different kind of quality, based on other tastes and the pleasures of a variety of interest groups.

In response to these concerns, some authorities are re-introducing the idea of local-content quotas in order to bolster the home industry against what is seen to be unfair competition and cultural imperialism. In Australia cable networks are required to make 10 percent of the content of their channels locally produced dramas. This is leading to some serious head scratching and some good results.

As concern is voiced about the survival of public-service broadcasting, the public is itself seen to be moving away from this sector. In the USA the public-service television sector is minute, and in Australia, whilst the public-service broadcaster ABC is strongly supported in theory, it suffers from audience apathy in the ratings (see right). In Europe, however, although individual commercial offerings top the ratings, and despite a widely and rapidly diversifying field of broadcasters, most of the large public broadcasters are maintaining a fairly steady audience share (see "TV in Europe" below right). In India government-sponsored channels have a far larger share than their commercial competitors (see right).

The big losers are, and will continue to be, the free-to-air commercial broadcasters, whose content is more directly challenged by the offerings of the cable and satellite companies. The main threats come from the increased choice and interactivity promised by companies using digital technologies (see *Digital TV* pages 52–53). For example, the current staple of "lifestyle programs", "talk shows" and "reality TV" in Australia, the USA and the UK, are associated with print spin-offs supplied by the organizations that own both the network and the publishing company. These shows have a good public share, and arguably support the commercial networks' overall popularity in their local regions. However, when digital streaming allows audiences to shop online, or to switch direct to a web page that contains additional information on the show, or skip certain adverts that do not appeal to them, what will happen to the current synergies in commercial media? If free-to-air networks re-invent themselves with hidden subscription strategies (immediate access to magazine contents online) and work to build advertising into the shows (without breaking local regulations), they might profit from the changes. Otherwise, they may disappear in the face of subscription flexibility.

TV IN AUSTRALIA
Top five programs
excluding sports
2000

1	Friends	commercial	foreign
2	Nine Renovation Rescue 2	commercial	Australian
3	Nine Renovation Rescue	commercial	Australian
4	Con Air	commercial	Australian
5	Backyard Blitz	commercial	Australian

The expansion of digital capability does, however, suggest that all providers – both public and commercial – can engage in enhanced activities. That depends on how much freedom governments allow them to invest in new formats and in researching audience reactions to those innovations. It is hard for small national companies to compete with large media magnates, who can bundle international cable packages from their existing network and cable content holdings in the USA. In the, still-small, satellite television sector the worldwide versions of Europe public broadcasters are moving into the picture, just as they have been highly present in radio offshore services. This can be understood as a valuable window on the world, or as colonization by benevolence – or as a mixture of the two.

In some places, television is public by virtue of its compliance with national regulations and national needs. In Australia, a multilingual society, the Special Broadcasting Service (SBS) produces high-quality programming on minority interest topics. In Singapore, also with an official multicultural

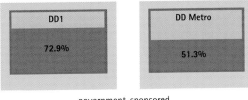

government-sponsored

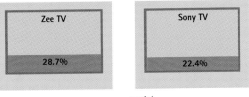

commercial

broadcasting remit, programs are provided in English, Chinese, Malay and Tamil. There are also brief forays into Singlish – a local, but officially unrecognized version of English – especially used by popular comedians. It would be hard for an overseas-based broadcaster to compete with such shows.

Television is important both as a medium of entertainment and for describing a nation to itself. Public-service broadcasting means something quite different in China (PRC), where "the national interest" is of prime concern in programming decisions. CCTV (Chinese Central Television) syndicates news programming and other content from its nine channels right across the spectrum of Chinese television delivery. Although the increasing number of cable channels (see *Satellite v Cable* pages 50–51) is already causing a boom in production, and a local focus for local cable services is likely to be a developing trend, the central State Administration of Film, Television and Radio is unlikely to release control over key ideological thematics.

One example of how the state control of television can backfire, however, occurred in Romania in the late 1980s. The President, Nicolae Ceaucescu, was concerned about the foreign influence of TV soaps and limited television broadcasting to two hours a day, axing the popular *Onedin Line* and *Dallas*. Romanians retaliated by buying extended aerials that gave them access to the soap operas on Hungarian television. They also picked up news of street demonstrations in Romania. The overthrow of the Ceaucescu government was hastened significantly by the up-to-date information gained from these broadcasts.

TV IN EUROPE

Trends in audience shares for public and commercial free-to-air terrestrial services between 1993 and 1998

- [ ] commercial
- [x] public

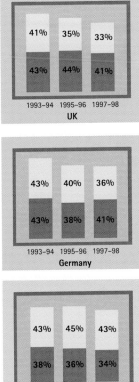

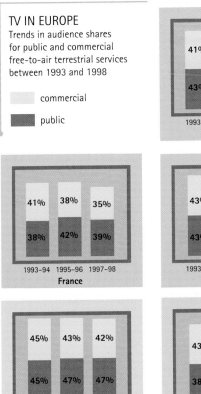

CABLE *v* SATELLITE

The worldwide distribution of cable and satellite infrastructure and services is not simply due to market demand. Terrain, demography, economic uncertainty, politics and regulations are all factors in national and local decisions to promote these forms of television delivery.

In Iran, the desire to exclude "politically inappropriate" content – especially that which contradicts the religious and moral beliefs of the country's government – informs strong regulatory decisions against satellite TV, although satellite dishes are bought on the black market. In Saudi Arabia over 60 percent of households enjoy regular access to satellite TV in an attempt to access a wider variety of programs than is available on government-run channels. In Singapore satellite dishes are restricted because the government favors terrestrial cable, whereby content is more easily controlled.

In China the huge growth in cable services (see *Television Worldwide* pages 46–47) is due in part to the government's desire to control content. The vast size of the country itself is another reason: cable is a relatively cheap way of connecting people in rural areas to local provincial TV stations. That said, one of the most poignant images of recent film in China was a peasant woman using her noodle basket as a free satellite dish on her tiny house. She had television, but she had lost the tools of her trade.

Satellite is valuable to populations of overseas Chinese who use it to receive CCTV4, an English–Chinese language channel produced in China especially for diasporic consumption. In India, DTH (direct-to-home) satellite has been held up by licensing problems, based on concerns of foreign takeover and foreign content in the domestic TV sphere. In 2000 foreign media companies were finally allowed a 20-percent share in DTH ownership and subscribers are expected to grow rapidly (see "Satellite TV subscribers in India").

Satellite markets in economically unstable areas, or areas beset by natural disaster, are difficult to predict. In the mid-1990s Rupert Murdoch's News Corp and Hughes' Electronic Corp invested US$2 billion in satellite TV in the expectation that 10 million Latin American households would buy the service. In 1999 Sky Latin America and Galaxy Latin America had fewer than 1.2 million subscribers and are unlikely to make a profit before 2002.

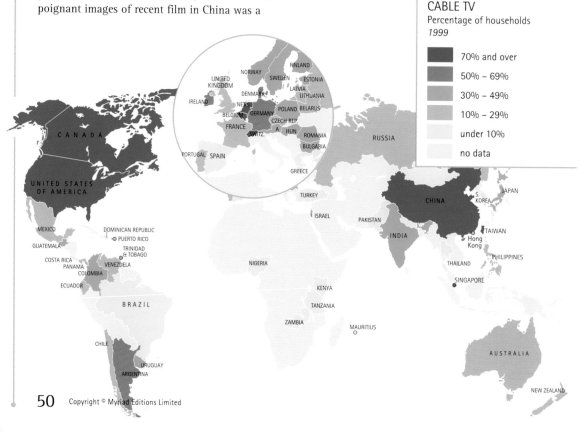

CABLE TV
Percentage of households
1999

- 70% and over
- 50% – 69%
- 30% – 49%
- 10% – 29%
- under 10%
- no data

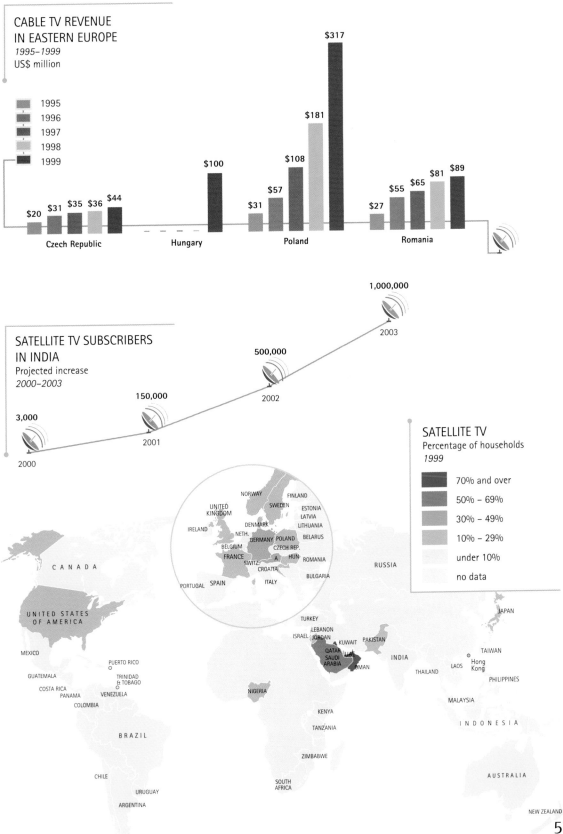

CABLE TV REVENUE IN EASTERN EUROPE
1995–1999
US$ million

- 1995
- 1996
- 1997
- 1998
- 1999

Czech Republic
$20 $31 $35 $36 $44

Hungary
$100

Poland
$31 $57 $108 $181 $317

Romania
$27 $55 $65 $81 $89

SATELLITE TV SUBSCRIBERS IN INDIA
Projected increase
2000–2003

3,000 — 2000
150,000 — 2001
500,000 — 2002
1,000,000 — 2003

SATELLITE TV
Percentage of households
1999

- 70% and over
- 50% – 69%
- 30% – 49%
- 10% – 29%
- under 10%
- no data

CANADA
UNITED STATES OF AMERICA
MEXICO
PUERTO RICO
GUATEMALA
COSTA RICA
PANAMA
TRINIDAD & TOBAGO
VENEZUELA
COLOMBIA
BRAZIL
CHILE
URUGUAY
ARGENTINA

NORWAY
FINLAND
UNITED KINGDOM
SWEDEN
ESTONIA
LATVIA
DENMARK
LITHUANIA
IRELAND
NETH.
GERMANY
POLAND
BELARUS
BELGIUM
CZECH REP.
FRANCE
SWITZ.
A
HUN
ROMANIA
CROATIA
PORTUGAL
SPAIN
ITALY
BULGARIA

RUSSIA
TURKEY
LEBANON
ISRAEL
JORDAN
KUWAIT
PAKISTAN
QATAR
SAUDI ARABIA
UAE
OMAN
INDIA

JAPAN
TAIWAN
Hong Kong
LAOS
THAILAND
PHILIPPINES
MALAYSIA

NIGERIA
KENYA
TANZANIA
ZIMBABWE
SOUTH AFRICA

INDONESIA
AUSTRALIA
NEW ZEALAND

51

DIGITAL TV

Television has reached a turning point. The technology is changing. Content can now be delivered by a number of different methods. Satellite TV and cable TV subscriptions have increased in most industrialized countries (see *Cable v Satellite* pages 50–51) and digital television (DTV) is taking over from the older analog model (see below). By 2003 DTV penetration throughout Western Europe is expected to increase to 33 percent of households, from only 7 percent in 1999, with 52 percent in the UK and 40 percent in Germany.

Digital technology enables more channels to be broadcast on a given bandwidth. It also allows for a high-definition picture quality, although this takes up more space on the bandwidth. Broadcasters and national governments are having to decide whether to privilege picture quality over diversity in their allocation of bandwidth resources. The media industry is giving the world advanced television services, such as High Definition Television (HDTV), and Standard Definition Television (SDTV), with better picture quality and sound and, in the most advanced services, links to the Internet and other online services. However, the USA has been slow to adopt HDTV, and countries such as the UK have opted for lower standards of picture and sound quality and less expensive "set-top boxes" for delivery of pay-TV services.

These changes are having a huge impact on the variety of programs on offer and on the uses to which we put our televisions. The extent to which television will be "interactive", with true "video on demand" and video tele-conferencing, will vary radically from country to country and even within a country. The present and near future for most of us is perhaps best described as "reactive television", in which we will be able to choose from menu lists, much as we already do on the Internet. Over the next two, five or ten years, television sets will be equally capable of showing your child's personal web page (with her own video productions) in high definition as the

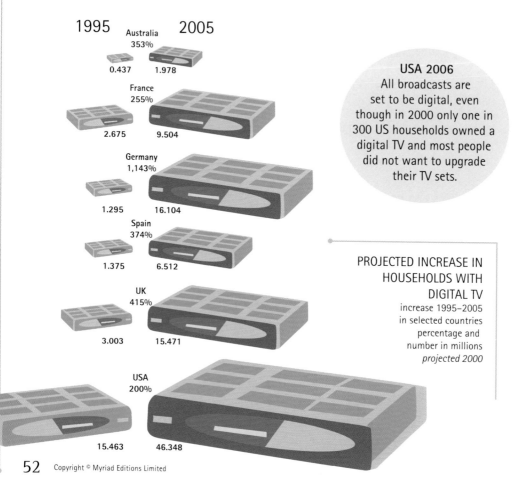

1995   2005

Australia
353%
0.437   1.978

France
255%
2.675   9.504

Germany
1,143%
1.295   16.104

Spain
374%
1.375   6.512

UK
415%
3.003   15.471

USA
200%
15.463   46.348

USA 2006
All broadcasts are set to be digital, even though in 2000 only one in 300 US households owned a digital TV and most people did not want to upgrade their TV sets.

PROJECTED INCREASE IN
HOUSEHOLDS WITH
DIGITAL TV
increase 1995–2005
in selected countries
percentage and
number in millions
projected 2000

A is for **Affiliate**
A station that carries a network's programs in return for a fee. In the USA this is a commercial arrangement. In China the same system works as a way of ensuring that state-sponsored national content reaches all of the people some of the time. All local stations carry CCTV (Chinese Central TV) main news bulletins.

B is for **Bandwidth**
The measure for the capacity of a television carrier.

C is for **Cable**
Cable television is delivered to homes by cables. Broadband carries 20 or more channels, narrowband carries fewer than ten.

D is for **DBS**
Direct Broadcast by Satellite, or DTH (Direct To Home): satellite signals transmitted direct to a dish on the domestic rooftop. Free-to-air providers also download material from around the world by satellite and then re-transmit to their audience.

E is for **Encryption**
Signal scrambling so that the code can be broken only by paying subscribers, often through a smart card.

F is for **Format TV**
Licensing program concepts to new markets via programmers, who use national languages, homegrown talent and content to make the show "local".

highlights of the latest sports spectacular. The provider of media content could be a multi-national network or a local community group.

Decision makers – and, to a certain extent, consumers – are faced with a series of choices, although as with any set of opposites, the context in which these choices are made is rarely straightforward. Real people, real consumers, and real purchasers often do not take to the new technology in the ways in which the forecasters expect. For example, in 1997 Microsoft bought WebTV for US$425 million. Three years later only one percent of US households had signed up for the service. Individual programming content was not the main issue, but rather the failure to understand how people like to use technology in their own homes.

CHOICES

Few channels	**1**	Many channels
Broadcasting: everyone sees the same program	**2**	Multicasting: customized information delivered to target groups
Broadcasting: large audiences for undifferentiated programs	**3**	Narrow casting: choice of schedule, pay-per-view
Mass programing	**4**	Niche programing
National audiences	**5**	Target – or niche – audiences
Inhouse production	**6**	Outsourced production
Free to Air: sourced by license, government funds, or advertising	**7**	Pay TV: pay-by-view, video-on-demand
Analog	**8**	Digital
Passive switch on / switch off	**9**	Interactive choose time and type of programing, shopping channels, language choices
Highly regulated	**10**	Less tightly regulated

TV RATINGS

Ratings – the measure of how many people watch a program – have always been cruelly important in the television business. They are especially important for free-to-air television services, where access to an audience is sold to advertisers, with programming as the bait to lure the viewers. Advertisers generally want as many as possible of the "right" kind of people to see their ads, and the broadcasters need to show them who will be watching. When public broadcasters are competing with these commercial stations, they need to demonstrate that they serve a substantial proportion of the total "viewing public" in order to justify government funding.

In the anxious new world of 21st-century television both commercial networks and public broadcasters face a long-term, and apparently irreversible, decline in audience numbers.

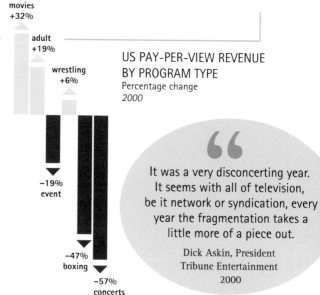

US PAY-PER-VIEW REVENUE BY PROGRAM TYPE
Percentage change
2000

movies +32%
adult +19%
wrestling +6%
–19% event
–47% boxing
–57% concerts

> " It was a very disconcerting year. It seems with all of television, be it network or syndication, every year the fragmentation takes a little more of a piece out.
>
> Dick Askin, President
> Tribune Entertainment
> 2000

CNN IN EUROPE
Percentage of top earners sampled who had viewed CNN in the previous 30 days
2000

- 50% – 59%
- 40% – 49%
- 30% – 39%
- 20% – 29%

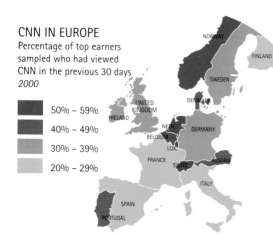

Free-to-air networks in the USA are losing market share – to cable television and to other media markets – but they are not about to disappear (see *Local v Global, Public v Commercial* pages 48-49). Competition for audience share is becoming both more complex and fierce. With an estimated 102.2 million television households in the USA, a single ratings point equals 1.02 million households – a prize worth fighting for. The end of the 20th century saw "reality television" boosting network ratings and revenues, and in the 21st century we will see the networks convincing advertisers that the "eyeballs" are still following them.

For pay-per-view audiences the price of a program largely relates to the viewer's

desire to watch it. Ratings in one sense then become less important, as one viewer willing to pay $10 to watch a program is as valuable as ten viewers only willing to pay $1. The demand for different types of program changes quite rapidly, however, and predicting those changes is essential to protect revenue (see above).

An increase in the number of channels requires more careful targeting. An accurate picture of the consumer lifestyles of more-segmented audiences is essential. Media providers are not only competing with each other but with time. There are only 24 hours in a day and as more media become available, there is only a limited amount of time to use them. With a wider range of media available in younger children's bedrooms, kids, tweens and teens are moving away from traditional TV networks. Increasingly intense lifestyle analysis of children by marketers will continue to shape the ratings landscape and the fate of the traditional networks.

EUROSPORT IN EUROPE
Percentage of top earners sampled who had viewed Eurosport in the previous 30 days
2000

- 60% – 69%
- 50% – 59%
- 40% – 49%
- 30% – 39%
- fewer than 30%

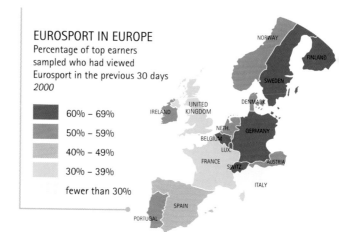

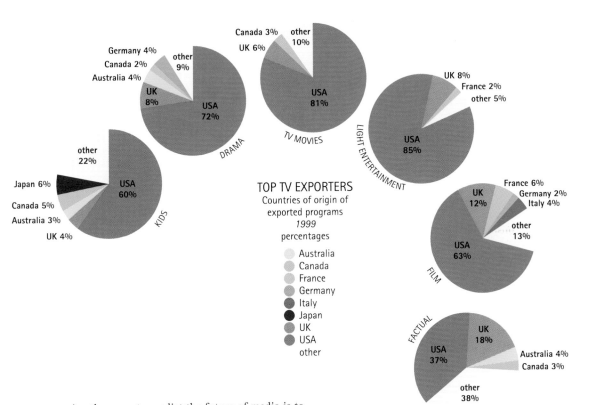

TOP TV EXPORTERS
Countries of origin of
exported programs
1999
percentages

- Australia
- Canada
- France
- Germany
- Italy
- Japan
- UK
- USA
- other

DRAMA
USA 72%
UK 8%
Australia 4%
Canada 2%
Germany 4%
other 9%

TV MOVIES
USA 81%
UK 6%
Canada 3%
other 10%

LIGHT ENTERTAINMENT
USA 85%
UK 8%
France 2%
other 5%

KIDS
USA 60%
UK 4%
Australia 3%
Canada 5%
Japan 6%
other 22%

FILM
USA 63%
UK 12%
France 6%
Germany 2%
Italy 4%
other 13%

FACTUAL
USA 37%
UK 18%
Australia 4%
Canada 3%
other 38%

Another way to predict the future of media is to see what the wealthiest sector of the population is up to. The European Media Survey, for example, samples the tastes and habits of 40 million key customers, across 16 European countries, whose incomes are in the top-20-percent bracket. The survey shows that the wealthy, traditionally "time poor", are moving to the international channels. CNN and Eurosport are a staple part of their media diet (see maps opposite), but smaller and less well-established channels are generating the highest percentage annual growth. The figures for 1998 and 1999 show BBC World up 37 percent, CNBC up 96 percent and Bloomberg up 191 percent.

Ratings are important not only for predicting national audiences but also for taking decisions about international audiences. *Baywatch*, the famous US soap, was a hit outside of the USA but received only a lukewarm reception in its home country. As the graphic above ("Top TV Exporters") shows, the USA and UK still dominate the TV export market.

Public broadcasters are also under pressure to show that they have an audience. It used to be assumed that something close to a 50-percent audience share gave a public-service broadcaster the status of a national broadcaster with a legitimate claim on the public purse. In the UK,

however, the BBC argues that ratings are only one form of feedback, and that qualitative criteria are needed to assess whether they are fulfilling their responsibility to produce quality programming and dependable news coverage, and to provide a forum for informed political debate.

Researchers analyse audiences' viewing habits by continuously surveying "panels" composed of thousands of households with "people-meters" installed to monitor viewing habits. These days, however, the focus is starting to shift from the measurement of "households" to the tracking of "individuals". Special wristwatches have been designed to collect data about where viewers go and what they do. Signals collected from the watches are matched against catalogued information of sounds and movements: analysts can then determine what viewers were watching when their attention wandered for long enough to make a drink or visit the bathroom, or whether their viewing was interrupted by a phone call.

HOME ENTERTAINMENT

VCRs (video-cassette recorders), video games, DVDs (originally called "digital versatile disks") and video cameras are all "time shifters", allowing us to organize our own entertainment, free from the constraints of scheduled broadcasts. We have become so used to this concept, so quickly, that we are now quite blasé about the control we have over viewing what we want, *when* we want it.

The VCR first made "time shifting" possible in the 1970s. For the first time people were able to record movies, their favorite shows, sports events or local news items for later viewing, and to keep them for posterity. The commercial value of such "time shifting" was quickly recognized, and video rental stores sprang up across the industrialized world. As this map shows, VCR sales in 1999 were still booming worldwide.

Pong, the first successful video game, reached US arcades in 1971. PacMan, Galaxian and Space Invaders followed. During the 1970s video games entered the home, with the first wave of video game businesses including Atari, Midway, Sega, Namco, Taito, Mattel and Cinematronics. In the 1990s Nintendo Entertainment System marked the second wave of video games, with its 8-bit video system. Sony PlayStation also emerged in the 1990s and in just a few years had joined Nintendo and Sega Dreamcast as household names. Early in 2001, however, Sega announced it was terminating production of Dreamcast. Its 9 million sales were no match for Nintendo's 30 million and Sony PlayStation's 76 million. A further 7 million sales of PlayStation II in just three months may have contributed to Sega's decision.

The first DVDs appeared in 1995 and the market is now growing at an astounding rate (see opposite). Similar to CD-Roms, DVDs have greater storage capacity, allowing videos to run from PCs. One consumer survey found that the average DVD owner is an entertainment enthusiast, most likely male, who also owns video games, a PC, at least two VCRs, subscribes to cable and spends more time on the Internet than non-DVD owners.

One of the effects of "time shifting" has been the loss of the sense of community created by everyone watching the same program at the same time. Television used to be considered as social cement, with families gathering round the

VCR ownership in the USA increased from 1.1% of households in 1980 to 85% in 1995

monitor, and nations sharing news and common cultural interests. It was a form of entertainment that did not require participation – unless you put your hand up for a game show. With the advent of video recorders and video games the television monitor became simply another medium for delivering a wide range of entertainment, and not as a vehicle for pre-ordained program schedules.

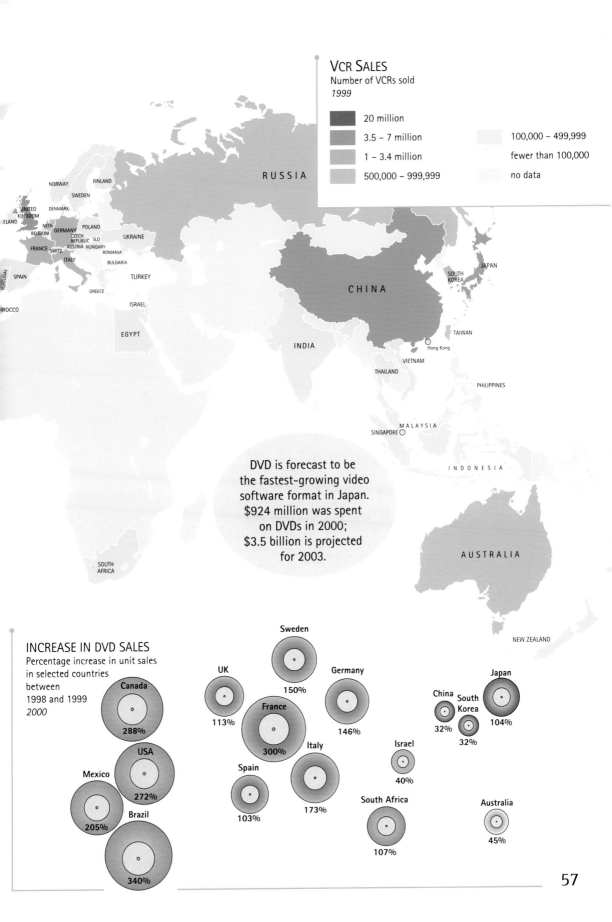

VCR SALES
Number of VCRs sold
1999

■ 20 million	
■ 3.5 – 7 million	☐ 100,000 – 499,999
■ 1 – 3.4 million	fewer than 100,000
☐ 500,000 – 999,999	no data

RUSSIA

NORWAY FINLAND
SWEDEN
UNITED DENMARK
KINGDOM
ELAND NETH. POLAND
BELGIUM GERMANY
CZECH SLO
REPUBLIC UKRAINE
FRANCE SWITZ. AUSTRIA HUNGARY
ITALY ROMANIA
BULGARIA
PORTUGAL
SPAIN TURKEY
GREECE
ISRAEL
ROCCO
EGYPT

CHINA

JAPAN
SOUTH
KOREA

TAIWAN
Hong Kong

INDIA

VIETNAM
THAILAND

PHILIPPINES

MALAYSIA
SINGAPORE

INDONESIA

SOUTH
AFRICA

AUSTRALIA

DVD is forecast to be
the fastest-growing video
software format in Japan.
$924 million was spent
on DVDs in 2000;
$3.5 billion is projected
for 2003.

NEW ZEALAND

INCREASE IN DVD SALES
Percentage increase in unit sales
in selected countries
between
1998 and 1999
2000

Canada 288%

USA 272%

Mexico 205%

Brazil 340%

UK 113%

Sweden 150%

France 300%

Germany 146%

Spain 103%

Italy 173%

Israel 40%

South Africa 107%

China 32%

South Korea 32%

Japan 104%

Australia 45%

OWNERSHIP AND CONTROL

350BC Postal system of horsemen in relay *Persian Empire*
500BC Postal system of map-guided runners *Chinese Empire*
632–1259 Surface mail by horse, airmail by pigeon *Islamic Empires*
1900–1945 Radio broadcasting *competing empires*
1989–2001 Star wars *US global domination*

MEDIA MOGULS

Twentieth-century industrial giants, such as Standard Oil, US Steel, General Motors, Boeing, and Westinghouse, produced *things* – oil, steel, cars, airplanes, household appliances.

The media, however, have always been in the business of *immaterial commodities*. The newspaper is less important than reading it, the reel of film is less important than watching the movie, the CD is less important than hearing the music. What we buy is access to information and to certain types of experience. Some economists believe that this characteristic presages a new Industrial Revolution. They foresee an increasingly *weightless* economy, in which immaterial commodities are produced by transitory teams (rather than permanent staff) using networked technologies (rather than a manufacturing plant).

There are two struggles in today's media and information economy. One is over content. Multiplying channels and new media demand ever more material, and much of it today is either recycled or cheap and shoddy. Hence the fierce competition for rights over the few genres that guarantee large audiences, notably successful feature films and high-profile sporting events. The other battle is about *access* to content. Here, technology is important. Producing a newspaper every day, building up a catalogue of books or records, releasing enough hit films to cover the flops, and keeping up a regular flow of radio or television broadcasting each required a different type of workforce, used different technologies and persuaded consumers to part with their money in its own way. Now that digital technologies are leading to a convergence between previously distinct modes of production and dissemination there is the potential for sharing a common distribution infrastructure with a global reach. The question then is, who will be the gatekeepers of that infrastructure and control consumers' access to it?

Corporations such as AOL Time Warner, Disney, Viacom, Bertelsmann, News Corporation, AT&T, General Electric and Seagram all have their sights set on global markets, public access, and exploitable archives of films, programming, music, and text. Each already achieves annual sales of between US$10 billion and US$30 billion. Although competitors, they come together to further common interests at particular moments, and then break apart again and reconfigure when political and economic circumstances change. With its shifting strategic alliances and jockeying for territorial advantage, the media and information economy resembles the intricate world of 19th-century politics, in which the major powers colonize markets, with consent if possible but resorting to gunboat diplomacy and hostile action when necessary. Already, these media powers are proving over-mighty for regulation by national laws.

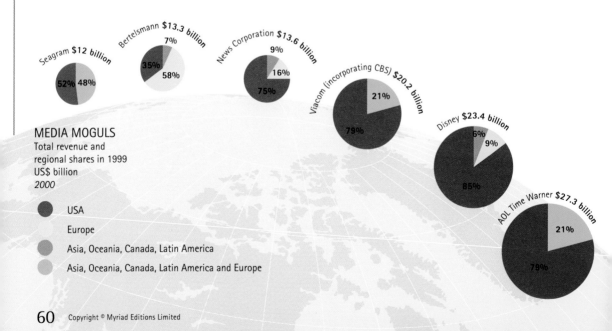

MEDIA MOGULS
Total revenue and
regional shares in 1999
US$ billion
2000

- USA
- Europe
- Asia, Oceania, Canada, Latin America
- Asia, Oceania, Canada, Latin America and Europe

Seagram $12 billion — 52% 48%

Bertelsmann $13.3 billion — 7% 35% 58%

News Corporation $13.6 billion — 9% 16% 75%

Viacom (incorporating CBS) $20.2 billion — 21% 79%

Disney $23.4 billion — 6% 9% 85%

AOL Time Warner $27.3 billion — 21% 79%

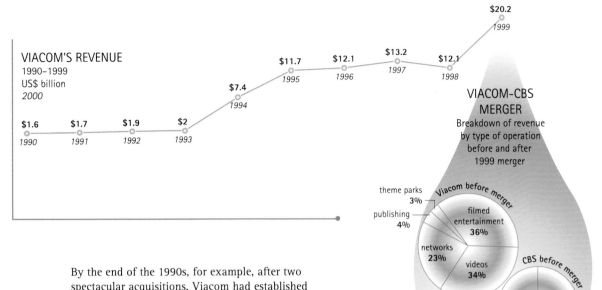

VIACOM'S REVENUE
1990–1999
US$ billion
2000

$1.6 — 1990
$1.7 — 1991
$1.9 — 1992
$2 — 1993
$7.4 — 1994
$11.7 — 1995
$12.1 — 1996
$13.2 — 1997
$12.1 — 1998
$20.2 — 1999

VIACOM-CBS
MERGER
Breakdown of revenue
by type of operation
before and after
1999 merger

Viacom before merger

theme parks 3%
publishing 4%
networks 23%
filmed entertainment 36%
videos 34%

CBS before merger

33%
Infinity (radio / outdoor advertising)
television / cable 67%

Viacom after merger with CBS

publishing 3%
theme parks 2%
radio / outdoor advertising 12%
videos 22%
filmed entertainment 22%
television / cable 39%

By the end of the 1990s, for example, after two spectacular acquisitions, Viacom had established itself as the fastest-growing media and entertainment corporation. When it was taken over in 1987 by the US cinema chain National Amusements, Viacom was running cable channels and making television programs. In the early 1990s, Paramount tried and failed to acquire Time Inc. Viacom moved in and took over the rebuffed Hollywood giant. The resulting conglomerate then controlled not just Paramount's catalogue of 50,000 films, but also Simon & Schuster's 300,000 book titles, Blockbuster's Video and Music stores, the Nickelodeon and MTV cable networks, as well as theme parks, television and radio stations, and cinema chains. When, in 1999, the US media regulator relaxed its rules on television ownership, Viacom took over the long-established television and radio networks of CBS (see right).

This US$36-billion merger created a third-generation Viacom and added to its existing revenue of over US$20 billion. In 1999 Viacom's advertising revenue of around US$11 billion accounted for four percent of the world total, nearly twice as much as that of its nearest rival, News Corporation. The twist to the story is that, before it was sold in 1970 as the result of an earlier regulatory decision, Viacom had been the production arm of a major media player — none other than the old CBS. The stories of the other leading firms, such as the merger between America Online and Time Warner and the expansion of the Disney and News Corp empires, are equally compelling (see pages 62–67).

The media economy operates globally, and yet the USA remains its center of gravity. The German company Bertelsmann, for example, is the largest European media conglomerate and concentrates its publishing and other activities in Europe. Although 28 percent of its revenue in 1999 came from Germany and 30 percent from the rest of Europe, 35 percent came from its US ventures, including publishing companies (Bantam Doubleday Dell and Random House), magazines (*Family Circle, McCall's* and *Parents*) and record labels (Arista and RCA). Other firms based outside the USA — such as the Canadian Seagram (until recently a drinks company, but now owner of Universal, PolyGram and other media holdings), the Australian News Corporation, and the Japanese Sony — also devote much of their energy to securing their position in the US market.

AOL Time Warner

When the publishing giant Time Inc took over Warner Communications Inc in January 1990, both parties justified it as a strategic response to globalization, which they saw "rapidly evolving from a prophecy to a fact of life". Time Warner's diversified operations included magazine and book publication, cable television systems, filmed entertainment and television programming, videos, music labels, cinema chains and theme parks. In 1996, Time Warner expanded further, acquiring Ted Turner's Turner Broadcasting System (TBS), whose CNN news channel reaches 200 million homes, hotels and other outlets in 212 countries. Time Warner took the opportunity to regroup its operations into filmed entertainment, cable networks, cable systems, publishing and music divisions.

America Online (AOL) has grown from a computer games supplier formed in 1983 to become the world's leading Internet service provider (ISP) when it acquired CompuServe in 1998. In 2000 it had over 22 million subscribers worldwide – a quarter of the world's Internet households, many of them in the affluent US market. Its revenues come from advertising, e-commerce, some business-to-business activities, and subscriptions – a legacy from the days of more cumbersome navigation, before free ISPs and open access became available.

AOL and Time Warner announced their intention to merge in January 2000. The reason was convergence between new and old media. The proposed company was valued at between $160 and $180 billion. By the end of the year, a volatile share market had seen that value fall to $75 billion.

What AOL saw in the deal was the promise of combining home information with home entertainment. It needed Time Warner's huge back catalogue of movies, music and the rest. This is ripe for repackaging as an inducement to keep subscribers within AOL's "walled garden", thereby cranking up advertising revenue. AOL was also no doubt aware that the new bandwidth coming on stream is owned not by ISPs like itself, but by the USA's big cablers – AT&T, Charter and Time Warner. Time Warner had experienced a frustrating time trying to establish its own online franchise, and AOL offered a

prestigious name, an established subscriber base and proven technology. It may also have seen the merger as a pre-emptive strike. AOL was the market leader, and companies like Disney or CBS no doubt were also eyeing this juicy prize.

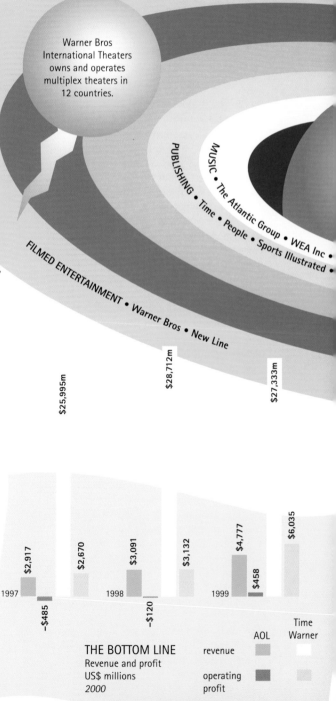

Warner Bros International Theaters owns and operates multiplex theaters in 12 countries.

PUBLISHING • Time • People • Sports Illustrated •

MUSIC • The Atlantic Group • WEA Inc •

FILMED ENTERTAINMENT • Warner Bros • New Line

$25,995m

$28,712m

$27,333m

$2,917

$2,670

$3,091

$3,132

$4,777

$6,035

$458

1997

1998

1999

–$485

–$120

THE BOTTOM LINE
Revenue and profit
US$ millions
2000

revenue

operating profit

AOL

Time Warner

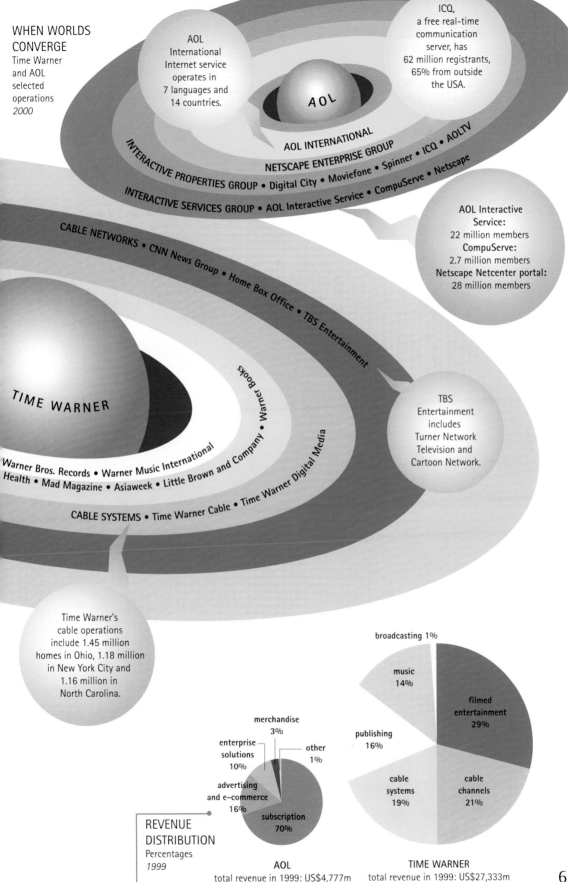

WHEN WORLDS CONVERGE
Time Warner and AOL selected operations 2000

AOL International Internet service operates in 7 languages and 14 countries.

ICQ, a free real-time communication server, has 62 million registrants, 65% from outside the USA.

AOL

AOL INTERNATIONAL

NETSCAPE ENTERPRISE GROUP

INTERACTIVE PROPERTIES GROUP • Digital City • Moviefone • Spinner • ICQ • AOLTV

INTERACTIVE SERVICES GROUP • AOL Interactive Service • CompuServe • Netscape

AOL Interactive Service: 22 million members
CompuServe: 2.7 million members
Netscape Netcenter portal: 28 million members

CABLE NETWORKS • CNN News Group • Home Box Office • TBS Entertainment

TIME WARNER

Warner Books

TBS Entertainment includes Turner Network Television and Cartoon Network.

Warner Bros. Records • Warner Music International
Health • Mad Magazine • Asiaweek • Little Brown and Company • Time Warner Digital Media

CABLE SYSTEMS • Time Warner Cable • Time Warner Digital Media

Time Warner's cable operations include 1.45 million homes in Ohio, 1.18 million in New York City and 1.16 million in North Carolina.

broadcasting 1%

music 14%

publishing 16%

filmed entertainment 29%

cable systems 19%

cable channels 21%

merchandise 3%

enterprise solutions 10%

other 1%

advertising and e-commerce 16%

subscription 70%

REVENUE DISTRIBUTION
Percentages 1999

AOL
total revenue in 1999: US$4,777m

TIME WARNER
total revenue in 1999: US$27,333m

63

DISNEY

Once upon a time, way back in the 1920s, there was a young animator named Walt Disney who started his own company making cartoon films about mischievous anthropomorphic animals with names like Mickey Mouse and Donald Duck. In one of the great 20th-century fairy tales, the small production company grew and grew until, by the end of the century, it had turned into a huge conglomerate with total revenue of over US$23 billion, a brand name and set of logos, characters and images that are known, loved and resented around the world.

Branding and cross-promotion – using one Disney commodity to advertise others – have sustained Disney's determined strategy of expansion and diversification since the new management team, led by Michael Eisner, arrived in 1984. "Team Disney" oversaw not only the clever exploitation of Disney's evergreen back catalogue, but also consolidation of existing activities and forays into new areas. In 1993, Disney reinforced its box-office clout by buying the successful independent distribution company Miramax. In 1995, it paid US$19 billion to acquire Capital Cities/ABC, thus adding an established, if slightly wobbly, television network to its own cable Disney Channel and the sports network ESPN. In the late 1990s, Disney made long-term investments in Internet and new media activities.

For all Disney's global recognition, its international theme parks and its hold over children's imaginations worldwide, a surprising 80 percent of its business is concentrated in the USA. The company created Walt Disney International in 1999, the aim of which is to raise per capita expenditure on Disney products in France, Germany, Italy, Japan and the UK to levels seen in the USA.

Disney thrives on synergy. If you watch a Disney channel, buy a Disney book or toy, visit Disneyland, or eat in a Disney restaurant, you will be bombarded with Disney imagery. A new brand may start as a cartoon feature backed up by toy merchandising, re-emerge as a television series, greet you in the theme parks, and turn up on Disney's websites. All the time, the brand and its Disney affiliation are hammered home, securing its cultural hold and increasing its value to the company.

STUDIO ENTERTAINMENT

film production:
- **Walt Disney Pictures**
- **Walt Disney Feature Animation**
- **Touchstone** • **Hollywood Pictures**
- **Caravan Pictures** • **Miramax Films**

television production:
- **Walt Disney Network Television**
- **Walt Disney Television Animation**

worldwide film distribution:
- **Buena Vista International**

recorded music production:
- **Buena Vista Music Group**

home video release:
- **Buena Vista Home Entertainment.**

In 2000, Disney won the highest share of the US domestic cinema market for the third year in succession.

Even so, Studio Entertainment's profits nose-dived.

1997	$1,079m
1998	$769m
1999	$116m

Buena Vista Home Entertainment was blamed. Its policy of releasing Disney classics only for limited periods – irritating both small children and harassed parents – is to be dumped.

THE BOTTOM LINE
Disney revenue and profit 1995–1999
US$ billion *2000*

	1995	1996	1997	1998	1999
revenue	$12.1	$18.7	$22.5	$23	$23.4
profit	$2.4	$3	$4.3	$4.1	$3.2

THEME PARKS AND RESORTS

- 7 theme parks
- 27 hotels
- 2 cruise ships

More punters are going through the turnstiles, and they are spending more. The division is booming, with annual profits increasing by almost 14%. In 2001, new sites were being built in the USA, Japan and France, despite a bumpy introduction for the first Disneyland Paris. Another is planned in Hong Kong.

BROADCASTING

Although Disney had television and radio interests before 1996, it was the acquisition of ABC that made broadcasting the heartland of the Disney empire. The deal delivered:

- the ABC television network
- 10 TV stations in US regional markets
- 5 radio news networks
- ESPN, a sports radio network
- Radio Disney, a children's radio network
- 42 radio stations
- ABC Television Entertainment Group, a program maker

CABLE

- 100% ownership of Disney Channel, Toon Disney and SoapNet
- 80% ownership of sports channel ESPN
- 50% ownership of Lifetime Television
- minority shares in E! Entertainment, A&E and The History Channel.

Although Disney's cable business is smaller than its broadcasting business, it is more profitable and it is growing at a faster rate, in line with the general trend in US television, as the networks grapple with declining audience figures and spiraling program production costs.

PUBLISHING

book publishers, including:
- **Walt Disney Book Publishing**
- **Hyperion**
- **Miramax Books**

four magazine publishing groups, including:
- **Women's Wear Daily**

11 newspapers, including:
- **St Louis Daily Record**
- **Daily Tidings** in Orlando
- **Oakland Press and Reminder**

HOW THE DISNEY COOKIE CRUMBLES
1999

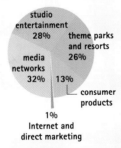

- studio entertainment 28%
- theme parks and resorts 26%
- media networks 32%
- 13% consumer products
- 1% Internet and direct marketing

SPORTS AND THEATRE

Walt Disney Theatrical Productions develops stage musicals, mostly based on Disney cartoon features, such as The Lion King and Beauty and the Beast. Disney also owns:

- **a National Hockey league team, the Mighty Ducks of Anaheim**

- **a share in a major league baseball franchise, the Anaheim Angels**

- **the Walt Disney World Sports Complex, which boasts a golf course, an auto racing track and baseball complex.**

NEW MEDIA

By the end of 1999, Disney had invested US $500 million in Internet activities, despite accumulating losses since 1997. Having bought the search engine Infoseek, Disney then merged it with the rest of its Internet and Direct Marketing division to create the new Disney-oriented portal **Go.com**. This also provides a domain name around which Disney's other websites are organized. Sites such as **disney.go.com, abc.go.com** and **espn.go.com** rank sixth in popularity among US users, attracting 23.1 million visitors in May 2000 alone.

NEWS CORPORATION

In the 1950s, the young Rupert Murdoch inherited an Australian newspaper called *The News* from his dad. Hardly a beginning in rags, but there is an epic quality to the buccaneering story of how he went on to build News Corporation into a global media empire.

From the 1950s until the late 1980s, Murdoch became an international press tycoon. In 1970s London, his populist *Sun* tabloid introduced the topless "Page 3 Girls" and had a pithy line in xenophobic headlines. In 1983 News Corporation launched Sky Television in the UK and, a couple of years later, acquired a crumbling pillar of the old Hollywood, Twentieth Century Fox. The Fox deal delivered not only production capacity, but also a way into US television via Twentieth Television. With the studio's catalogue and its own news-gathering expertise behind it, Fox took on the established networks, acquiring a network of stations and affiliates across the USA. Rather than competing for overall audience share, Fox cleverly targeted 18- to 49-year-old viewers with programs such as *The Simpsons*, *The X-Files* and *Ally McBeal*.

Rupert Murdoch has always understood the importance of content. Fox movies were useful. But his canniest instinct was to grasp the value of exclusive live coverage of sporting events. In the UK, BSkyB prospered only after winning the rights to the cream of English football in 1993. In the same year, Fox snared the rights to NFC American football from CBS. By 1998, Fox's top ten programs were all sporting events, six of them featuring in the national chart. A 30-second advertising spot during Fox's broadcast of the Superbowl in 1999 cost between US$2 million and US$3 million. In 2000, in Australia, Murdoch added the rights to Australian Rules football to his controlling share in the National Rugby League Championship.

New plotlines are appearing in the saga of News Corporation. Some concern Murdoch's health, private life and the dynastic transfer of power. Others concern his empire's continuing global spread, especially the attempt to establish Star TV and its Chinese partners as a trans-Asian force. Finally, like its competitors, News Corporation is nervously exploring how its creator's populist nose for content might be translated to the new media environment.

> **Our underlying philosophy is that all media are one. The principles and skills involved in discovering and fostering creative talent... are transferable.**
> Rupert Murdoch, 1987

CANADA

UNITED STATES OF AMERICA

Los Angeles Dodgers (baseball team) | Fox Broadcasting Company, Twentieth Televison | Twentieth Century Fox | Fox Sport Radio Network | *New York Post* | HarperCollins

LATIN AMERICA

Sky Latin America
Canal Fox
Fox Kids

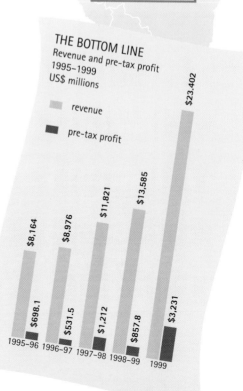

THE BOTTOM LINE
Revenue and pre-tax profit
1995–1999
US$ millions

■ revenue
■ pre-tax profit

1995–96	1996–97	1997–98	1998–99	1999
$8,164	$8,976	$11,821	$13,585	$23,402
$698.1	$531.5	$1,212	$857.8	$3,231

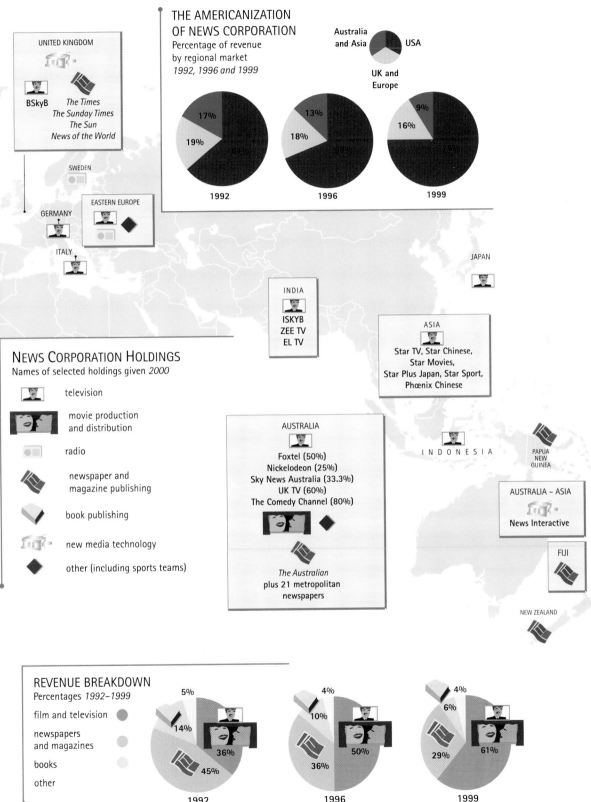

THE AMERICANIZATION OF NEWS CORPORATION

Percentage of revenue by regional market
1992, 1996 and 1999

Australia and Asia · USA · UK and Europe

1992: 17%, 19%, 64%
1996: 13%, 18%, 69%
1999: 9%, 16%, 75%

UNITED KINGDOM

BSkyB
The Times
The Sunday Times
The Sun
News of the World

SWEDEN

GERMANY

EASTERN EUROPE

ITALY

JAPAN

INDIA
ISKYB
ZEE TV
EL TV

ASIA
Star TV, Star Chinese,
Star Movies,
Star Plus Japan, Star Sport,
Phœnix Chinese

NEWS CORPORATION HOLDINGS
Names of selected holdings given *2000*

- television
- movie production and distribution
- radio
- newspaper and magazine publishing
- book publishing
- new media technology
- other (including sports teams)

AUSTRALIA
Foxtel (50%)
Nickelodeon (25%)
Sky News Australia (33.3%)
UK TV (60%)
The Comedy Channel (80%)

The Australian
plus 21 metropolitan
newspapers

INDONESIA

PAPUA NEW GUINEA

AUSTRALIA – ASIA
News Interactive

FIJI

NEW ZEALAND

REVENUE BREAKDOWN
Percentages *1992–1999*

- film and television
- newspapers and magazines
- books
- other

1992: 5%, 14%, 36%, 45%
1996: 4%, 10%, 50%, 36%
1999: 4%, 6%, 61%, 29%

67

ADVERTISING

The "social grades" used in advertising data in
the UK still distinguish types of household
by old-fashioned class categories.
Widows and state pensioners come
last in the pecking order.

THE ADVERTISING INDUSTRY

Newspapers and magazines have long combined the business of providing news, public information, and opinion with the opportunity to sell goods, services, and institutions. With the advent of radio and, later, of television in the USA, broadcasters quickly became dependent on this new and lucrative source of revenue.

The advertising industry develops rapidly. In young market economies, such as China and Russia, television stations, still state-managed, carry vast quantities of advertising, knowing that this source of revenue will fund public broadcasting beyond the resources of government.

Globally, new technologies have provided advertisers with the latest platform and means of mass communication. The growth in Internet advertising revenue has been dramatic: in 1999 it totalled $4.62 billion, an increase of 141 percent on the previous year.

Web advertising is still new, however, and remains a small proportion of the total advertising expenditure across different media. Despite the possibilities of the Internet, producers are keen to establish a profile in traditional public media before turning to the relative seclusion of the domestic personal computer. Direct mail, print media, telephone contact, billboards and broadcast television continue to lead the way in outreach, design, and impact.

Newspaper and magazine advertisements still dominate in developed countries in Europe and in Asia, as well as in the USA. Developing countries are also investing in press advertising. Often producers want to focus on local audiences rather than on global markets. An advertisement placed in a national paper can be run in the national language and use colloquialisms, shared humor and local knowledge to persuade the consumer to buy the product. This kind of detail is harder to achieve in an online advertisement which, though potentially reaching a wider audience, may lack the "bite" of the pun or quip that ultimately sells the product.

Some products already enjoy a global outreach – brand names such as Disney, Mattel, and Warner, for example. These major media players were quick to harness the Web to deepen their market penetration, and recognized that investing in online advertising would expand their global scope and recognition.

They were also amongst the first to exploit one of the fastest-growing markets.

Over 90% of television viewers misunderstand between 25% and 30% of any broadcast. They are less likely to misunderstand advertising, than entertainment and news programs.

In Bahrain, Iceland, Nigeria, Norway, Portugal and Thailand, the law forbids or restricts the use of women simply to attract attention in advertisements unless the product is relevant for women as consumers.

ADVERTISING IN THE USA

Annual expenditure and
percentage growth
US$ millions
1997–1998

Expenditure	Growth	Medium
$1.9	112%	Internet
$10.4	13%	cable TV
$1.6	8%	outdoor
$14.6	8%	radio
$39.7	8%	direct mail
$39.5	7%	broadcast TV
$4.4	7%	business papers
$25.5	7%	miscellaneous
$44.3	6%	newspapers
$10.4	6%	magazines
$12.0	5%	yellow pages
$0.3	5%	farm pubs

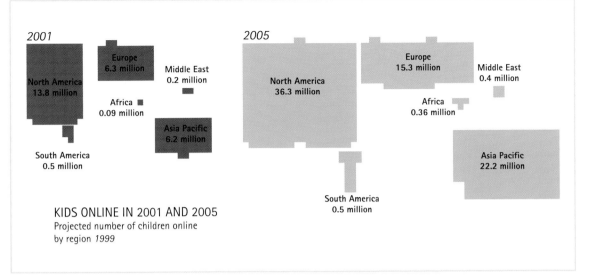

2001

North America
13.8 million

Europe
6.3 million

Middle East
0.2 million

Africa
0.09 million

South America
0.5 million

Asia Pacific
6.2 million

2005

North America
36.3 million

Europe
15.3 million

Middle East
0.4 million

Africa
0.36 million

Asia Pacific
22.2 million

South America
0.5 million

KIDS ONLINE IN 2001 AND 2005
Projected number of children online
by region *1999*

By 2005 the number of children online is projected to increase by 400 percent. To attract these new young consumers, some producers are pushing advertising in interesting directions, especially through interactivity. On the Barbie site, for example, visitors are invited to design their own doll and then buy her.

Globally, only 8 percent of users cite buying online as a reason for using the Internet. Most – some 56 percent of Internet users worldwide – are searching for information; 38 percent are looking for work, and 36 percent using it for learning. There are more Internet shoppers in the USA than elsewhere but still they make up only 12 percent of total users.

www.nick.com	20%
www.pokemon.com	16.9%
www.cartoonnetwork.com	15.9%
www.nickjr.com	13.9%
www.lego.com	13.1%
www.antagonist.com	12.4%
www.broderbund.com	12%
www.gameshark.com	11.8%
www.nsync.com	11.3%
www.yahooligans.com	9.8%

TOP TEN WEBSITES FOR CHILDREN
Children aged 2 to 11 as a percentage
of all visitors to the site *December 1998*

ADVERTISING EXPENDITURE

Advertising in newspapers and magazines has remained dominant in world markets, despite the rapid growth of Internet advertising.

UNITED KINGDOM 6.6%

1%
4%
4%
33%
40%
18%

CANADA **1.9%**

IRELAND

FRANCE 3.7%

1%
11%
7%
24%
34%
23%

UNITED STATES
OF AMERICA
43%

1%
13%
37%
37%
12%

SPAIN 1.9%

PORTUGAL
0.4%

PUERTO RICO
0.5%

COSTA RICA   PANAMA
0.7%   **0.7%**

COLOMBIA
1.1%   VENEZUELA
0.5%

PERCENTAGE OF TOTAL ADVERTISING EXPENDITURE IN DIFFERENT MEDIA
selected countries *1998*

outdoor   newspapers

cinema   magazines

radio   tv

BRAZIL
2.5%

ARGENTINA
1.3%

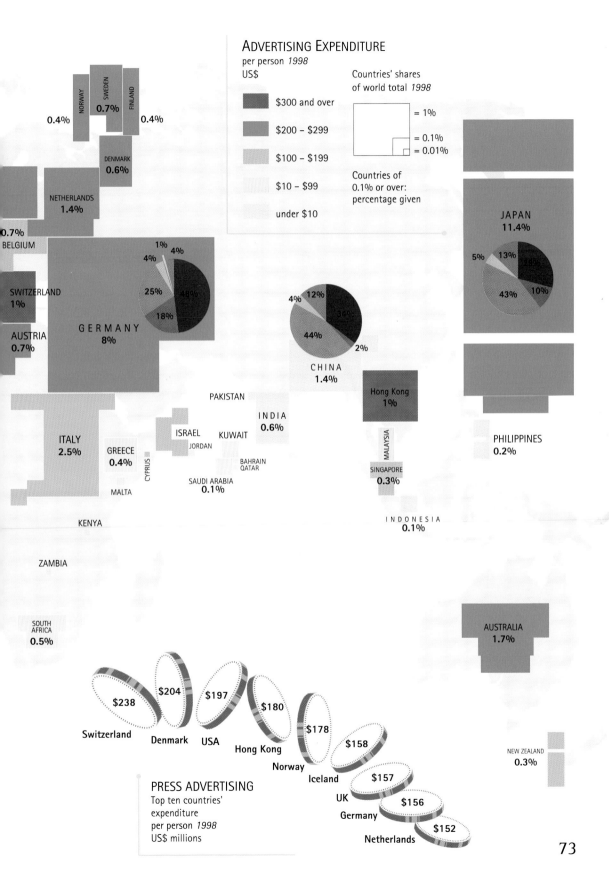

ADVERTISING EXPENDITURE

per person *1998*
US$

- $300 and over
- $200 – $299
- $100 – $199
- $10 – $99
- under $10

Countries' shares
of world total *1998*

= 1%
= 0.1%
= 0.01%

Countries of
0.1% or over:
percentage given

NORWAY 0.4%
SWEDEN 0.7%
FINLAND 0.4%
DENMARK 0.6%
NETHERLANDS 1.4%
0.7%
BELGIUM
SWITZERLAND 1%
AUSTRIA 0.7%
GERMANY 8%
ITALY 2.5%
GREECE 0.4%
CYPRUS
MALTA
KENYA
ZAMBIA
SOUTH AFRICA 0.5%

PAKISTAN
ISRAEL
JORDAN
KUWAIT
BAHRAIN
QATAR
SAUDI ARABIA 0.1%
INDIA 0.6%
CHINA 1.4%
Hong Kong 1%
MALAYSIA
SINGAPORE 0.3%
INDONESIA 0.1%

JAPAN 11.4%
PHILIPPINES 0.2%
AUSTRALIA 1.7%
NEW ZEALAND 0.3%

PRESS ADVERTISING

Top ten countries'
expenditure
per person *1998*
US$ millions

$238 Switzerland
$204 Denmark
$197 USA
$180 Hong Kong
$178 Norway
$158 Iceland
$157 UK
$156 Germany
$152 Netherlands

73

ADVERTISING STANDARDS

There are various levels of constraint exercised over the advertising industry. In a few countries the government imposes legal constraints. In general, the advertising companies regulate themselves, banning certain products or scenarios. Even where no formal regulations exist, advertisers in most countries exercise self-censorship, based on assumptions about what is deemed acceptable by the public.

Other forms of constraint arise from public protest against what is perceived as a logo-led culture and the increasing global domination of multinationals. In June 2000 computer hackers broke into Nike's website to protest against the company's alleged sweatshop practices. They redirected visitors to a protest site about globalization. The practise of parodying ads and hijacking web pages has been termed "culture jamming".

In 1995, Guinness launched an advertisement featuring a homosexual kiss. In the ensuing furore it was never aired. In 1998 that taboo was broken when a gay couple appeared in a "close encounter" for Impulse. A perfume advertisement featuring a naked model, displayed in the UK and Europe at the end of 2000, was banned by the UK Advertising Standards Authority on the grounds of being sexually suggestive and degrading to women. There was debate, however, as to whether a photograph of a lone woman in an apparent state of sexual excitement was a blow for or against feminism.

Restrictions on advertising include everything from "anti-clutter" codes relating to the siting of advertising boards, to outright bans of tobacco advertising in various media. Some societies also regulate their advertising by restricting the use of foreign language advertisements or requiring modifications for the local context.

The map illustrates how national advertising federations and associations rate various media – including broadcast television, cable, radio, newspapers, general magazines, women's magazines, men's magazines, posters, billboards and hoardings, and direct mail – in terms of accepting controversial advertisements. Their response was ranked on a four-point scale: from "very tolerant" to "very conservative".

Sexual violence against women in advertisements is deemed unacceptable everywhere except Argentina, Paraguay and Thailand.

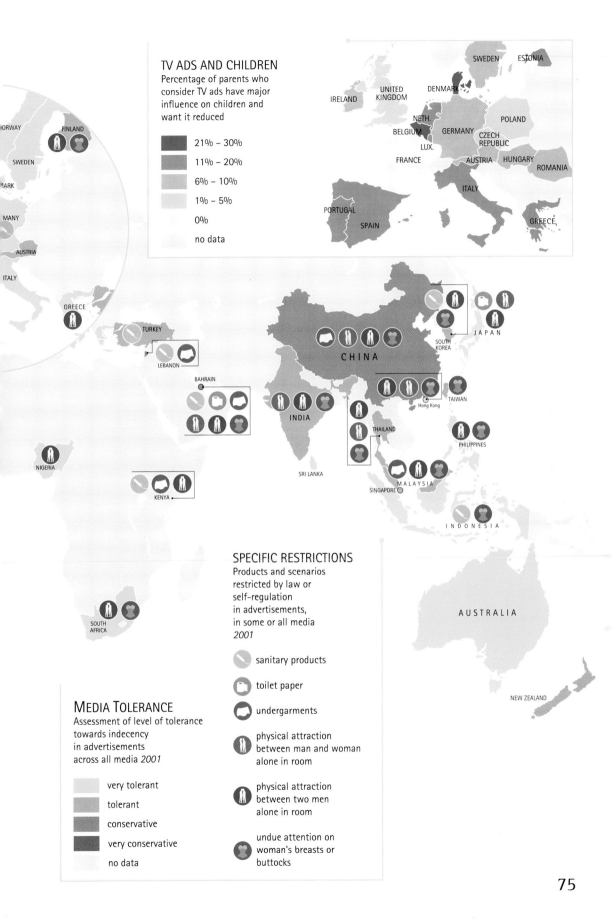

TV ADS AND CHILDREN
Percentage of parents who consider TV ads have major influence on children and want it reduced

- 21% – 30%
- 11% – 20%
- 6% – 10%
- 1% – 5%
- 0%
- no data

SPECIFIC RESTRICTIONS
Products and scenarios restricted by law or self-regulation in advertisements, in some or all media 2001

- sanitary products
- toilet paper
- undergarments
- physical attraction between man and woman alone in room
- physical attraction between two men alone in room
- undue attention on woman's breasts or buttocks

MEDIA TOLERANCE
Assessment of level of tolerance towards indecency in advertisements across all media 2001

- very tolerant
- tolerant
- conservative
- very conservative
- no data

75

INFORMATION AND COMMUNICATION TECHNOLOGIES

In January 2001 the average home Internet user spent nearly 3 hours a week surfing the Web and accessed 177 pages. The average work user spent nearly 5 and a half hours surfing and accessed 335 pages.

Plain Old Telephone Systems

In February 1876, Alexander Graham Bell filed an application with the US Patent Office for an "electric-speaking telephone". In the UK the first exchange opened in London in 1879 with fewer than ten subscribers, growing by 1887 to 26,000 subscribers. In the USA and the UK telephone use really became widespread only after World War II. By 1984 there were 30 million telephones in the UK; in 2000 over 90 percent of homes had at least one.

The Plain Old Telephone Service (or POTS, as it is affectionately known) is delivered by the Public Switched Telephone Network – a century-old network of access lines, trunks and switches crisscrossing the globe to provide affordable local and international calls.

In recent years, the "narrowband" POTS has been supplemented by sophisticated "broadband" services that carry more information and more diverse types of information, faster. In 1960 a transatlantic telephone cable could carry 138 conversations simultaneously. Today, a fiber-optic cable can deal with one and a half million voice conversations, as well as video, graphic and text signals. Broadband, or hybrid, services have made Internet use an everyday reality.

These expensive new networks remain unevenly distributed, even within industrialized countries. A telecommunications executive in the mid-1990s mischievously claimed that his company was interested only in 100 acres of the globe: the central business districts of New York, London, Tokyo, Frankfurt and other world cities. Here were their only profitable customers – 120 multinational companies. An exaggeration, maybe, but also a reminder that the expansion of telephone services is driven by the logic of profit rather than utopian dreams of a global village.

The pattern of telephone ownership and use is heavily skewed towards the advanced industrial nations. POTS, not the information superhighway, remains the measure for basic telecommunications provision. The urban legend is true. Well over 50 percent of the world's population have never made a phone call and live further than five kilometers from a traditional telephone service.

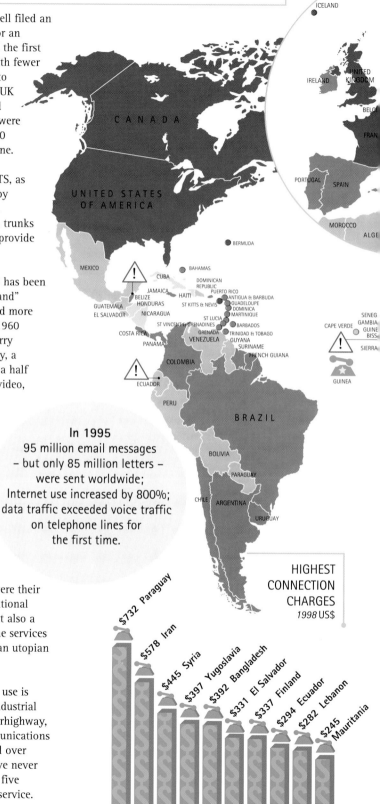

In 1995
95 million email messages
– but only 85 million letters –
were sent worldwide;
Internet use increased by 800%;
data traffic exceeded voice traffic
on telephone lines for
the first time.

HIGHEST
CONNECTION
CHARGES
1998 US$

$732 Paraguay
$578 Iran
$445 Syria
$397 Yugoslavia
$392 Bangladesh
$331 El Salvador
$337 Finland
$294 Ecuador
$282 Lebanon
$245 Mauritania

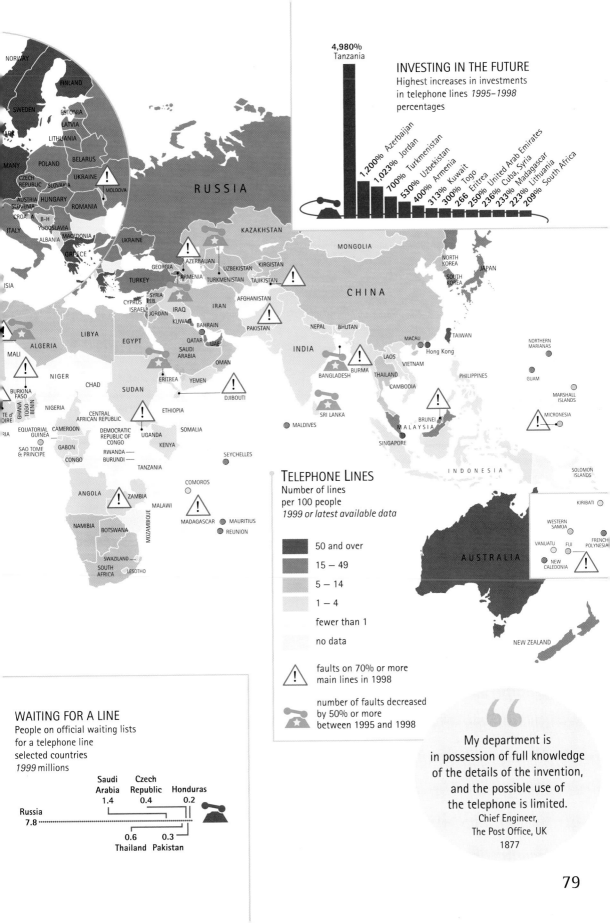

INVESTING IN THE FUTURE

Highest increases in investments in telephone lines *1995–1998* percentages

4,980% Tanzania
1,200% Azerbaijan
1,023% Jordan
700% Turkmenistan
530% Uzbekistan
400% Armenia
313% Kuwait
300% Togo
266 Eritrea
250% United Arab Emirates
236% Cuba, Syria
233% Madagascar
223% Lithuania
209% South Africa

TELEPHONE LINES

Number of lines per 100 people
1999 or latest available data

- 50 and over
- 15 – 49
- 5 – 14
- 1 – 4
- fewer than 1
- no data

⚠ faults on 70% or more main lines in 1998

☎★ number of faults decreased by 50% or more between 1995 and 1998

WAITING FOR A LINE

People on official waiting lists for a telephone line
selected countries
1999 millions

Russia 7.8
Saudi Arabia 1.4
Czech Republic 0.4
Honduras 0.2
Thailand 0.6
Pakistan 0.3

> My department is in possession of full knowledge of the details of the invention, and the possible use of the telephone is limited.
> Chief Engineer,
> The Post Office, UK
> 1877

79

CELL PHONES

Bangladesh, with only one fixed-line telephone for every 300 people, is the home of the phone lady. She makes her living by helping the poor connect to the rest of the world by cellular phone. Phone ladies buy their expensive phones using loans from Grameen Bank. Farmers use the phones to check on prices. Villagers use the phones to check on relatives. Between 1998 and 2000 the bank has supplied over 300 villages with phones. It plans to have a cellular phone within two kilometers of everyone in the country.

Cell phones are a "bypass technology". They allow people to connect to the digital world without the traditional telephone lines and terrestrial infrastructure. China, for example, where telephone lines are few and far between, has more subscribers than anywhere except the USA, and the average Chinese subscriber chats for over 400 minutes a month – three times longer than the average American.

Cell phones are also a "world in your pocket" technology. Cheap "power carrots" are designed for nothing other than chatting; "pocket boards" enable you to swap short text messages, and "smart phones" allow you do everything from keeping an address book to checking your email or sending pictures through a tiny digital camera. Wap phones, designed to expand the use of the Internet beyond the personal computer, have been slow to catch on, however.

Competition and liberalization affect cell-phone adoption. In 1999 Lebanon had the lowest prices at 7 cents a minute against a North African and Middle East regional average of 40–50 cents; charges in Norway dropped by 60 percent and in Germany by 70 percent. Conversely, in most of Latin America, where governments maintain monopolies on networks, prices stayed high – as much as ten times the cost of a local call. Despite this, the market there was buoyant (see "Mobile markets" opposite).

By 2004 World revenue from cell phones is expected to exceed fixed-line phone revenue.

CELL PHONE SALES
Unit sales 1995–1999 in millions
2000

Asia
9.4 (1995) 16 (1996) 21.3 (1997) 24.8 (1998) 30 (1999)

North America
11.5 (1995) 13.2 (1996) 14.5 (1997) 16.9 (1998) 18.2 (1999)

Western Europe
11.7 (1995) 16.3 (1996) 26.3 (1997) 41.2 (1998) 62 (1999)

In 2001
Over 50% of Europeans and 80% of Finns owned a cell phone.

CELL PHONES
Number per 1,000 people
1998

- more than 250
- 101 – 250
- 51 – 100
- 11 – 50
- 10 or fewer
- no data

In 2000
690 million people worldwide owned cell phones. One billion subscribers are expected by the end of 2002.

UK 2000
76% of 18-24 year olds and 43% adults used short text messaging.

MOBILE MARKETS
Percentage change in sales of cell phones
2000

- 1995–96
- 1996–97
- 1997–98
- 1998–99

North America
14.8%
9.8%
16.5%
7.7%

Brazil
35.2%
16.9%
60.2%

Western Europe
39.3%
61.3%
56.6%
50.5%
165.1%

Eastern Europe
120%
118%
91.6%
56.6%

Asia
70.2%
33.1%
16.4%
21%

Australia
40.3%
-2.6%
-3.1%
21.9%

South Africa
75.7%
63.9%
28%
38.4%

81

TELCOS

Until the 1980s, telecommunications services, or telecoms, were traditionally provided by a single operator holding a national monopoly. In the UK, the telephone system had long been part of the communications monopoly held by the Post Office (GPO), until British Telecom (BT) was created. Like most European operators, this was publicly owned. In the USA, AT&T (often called Ma Bell) was privately owned but regulated in the public interest.

In the 1980s, advances in information technology and services, combined with the passion for privatization shared by President Ronald Reagan in the USA and Prime Minister Margaret Thatcher in the UK, led to new experiments in telecoms

than 150 operators to operate in the UK, including AT&T.) Cable firms have used the capacity of their fiber optic lines to carry telephone signals (as well as television and the Internet) to challenge established telcos. Wireless telecoms services, such as cell phones, have been used by governments as Trojan horses to provoke greater competition. Although the established players have remained dominant in national telephone networks – the local loop that links individual customers to their local exchange – competitive pressures have driven up the quality of services. At the same time, the growing number of cell-phone subscribers and the narrowing cost differentials between cell-phone and fixed-line network services have intensified the pressure to reduce

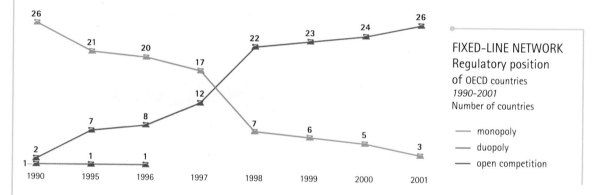

FIXED-LINE NETWORK
Regulatory position
of OECD countries
1990-2001
Number of countries

— monopoly
— duopoly
— open competition

regulation. In 1982, the US Consent Decree saw AT&T floating off its local operating companies – creating independent "Baby Bells" – in exchange for a looser regulatory regime allowing it to take advantage of convergence between telecoms and IT. In the UK, the British Telecommunications Act of 1981 privatized BT, licensed Mercury as its first competitor, and liberalized the market in telephone sets, cordless phones, fax machines, voice mail and other equipment. Crucially, the Act also followed the US precedent and created an independent public regulator (Oftel) to monitor competition and prices and to ensure that telecommunications companies, or telcos, meet their universal service obligations: to make their services accessible to the whole population at constant prices.

Since then, the number of telcos, the range of their activities and the scope of competition have all increased. (By 1996, Oftel had licenced more

prices. Worldwide, between 1996 and 1999, the price of telecoms services to consumers decreased on average by nearly 40 percent.

The experience of the USA and the UK encouraged others to mix market competition with public regulation. In 1987, the European Union declared its intention to liberalize telecoms, starting off with the easier bits, such as consumer

UNBUNDLING
Date of expected "unbundling"
for countries still controlled
by national networks
at the beginning of 2001

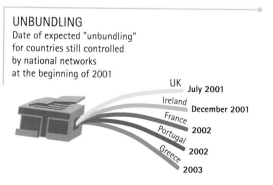

UK — July 2001
Ireland — December 2001
France — 2002
Portugal — 2002
Greece — 2003

82

equipment and new services, and moving to completely open markets by 1998. A 1999 report found, however, that "unbundling" local loops previously controlled by national networks by exposing them to competition from cable companies or cell-phone operators was going more slowly than planned, with some national regulators finding excuses for delay.

New possibilities opened up for US telcos with the Telecommunications Act in 1996. This further loosened regulation and allowed the Baby Bells and cable companies to move into the media field and strike alliances with Hollywood studios, television corporations and software companies (see *Media Moguls* pages 60–61). The prize now

the benefits of a technology revolution to citizens around the world". Instead, the pact accelerated the pace of mergers and acquisitions on a global scale, and hastened the likely domination of the world's telecoms market by a handful of telco giants. The frenetic operations of the telecoms market in 2000 were played out against the backdrop of the proposed mega-merger between America Online and Time Warner (see *AOL Time Warner* pages 62–63). The year started with telcos full of reckless enthusiasm. It ended more soberly, with growing concerns over revenues, debt loads and a slowing world economy. Even AT&T cut its dividend to shareholders by 87 percent, the first time it had done so since dividends were introduced in 1887.

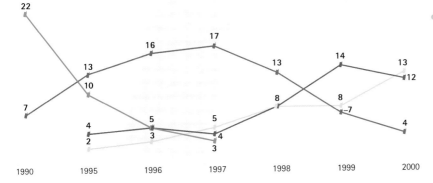

CELL-PHONE NETWORK
Regulatory position
of OECD countries
1990-2000
Number of countries

— monopoly
— duopoly
— 3 operators
— 4 or more operators

1990 1995 1996 1997 1998 1999 2000

is to control the content as well as the means of delivering information to individual consumers. With the ink on the Telecommunications Act scarcely dry, the telco US West bought Continental Cablevision, the third-largest cable system – only to be swallowed up itself by Qwest in July 1999. SBC Communications snapped up both Ameritech and PacBell and teamed up with BellSouth, to create Cingular. Bell Atlantic acquired Nynex and GTE, renamed itself Verizon and bought Vodafone, creating the country's leading wireless network.

In 1997, one year after the Telecommunications Act, the Global Telecommunications Agreement was brokered by the World Trade Organization and signed by 60 countries. The Agreement was designed to end state monopolies and to open the global market to international competition by allowing foreign investment in domestic telecoms. Its impact has not borne out then US President Bill Clinton's hope that the Agreement would "spread

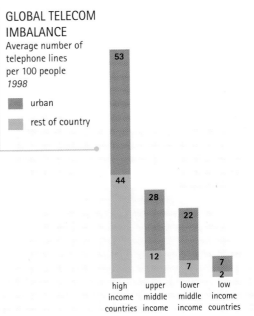

GLOBAL TELECOM IMBALANCE
Average number of telephone lines per 100 people
1998

■ urban
■ rest of country

high income countries
upper middle income
lower middle income
low income countries

INTERNET CONNECTIONS

The Internet brings together satellite and telephone communication with multimedia – sound, text and video. It has revolutionized the way we shop, and the nature of our leisure time.

These changes have happened with extraordinary speed. One of today's laptops offers processing power that 25 years ago was available only through a mainframe computer that filled a huge room and was affordable only by large corporations or the richest millionaire. The last "unconnected" country joined the Internet in 1998. By the end of 2000 the number of people online around the world was between 360 million and 380 million.

The distribution of the world's online population is uneven. More than 97 percent of all Internet hosts are in developed countries that are home to only 16 per cent of the world's population. Iceland, for example, with a population of only 250,000, has 20 times as many Internet hosts as the world's 100 poorest countries combined.

Global differences are mirrored in Internet use within the USA. Half the US population earning over $75,000 use the Internet at home, compared with fewer than 10 percent of those earning $25,000 or less. People with only high school qualifications or lower rarely use the Internet. Over 45 percent of those with a university degree or higher academic qualification use the Internet at home.

The Internet is not just a toy for boys. At home, 24 percent of US men use the Internet, and 21 percent of women. Outside the home, the comparison is 18 percent of men to 16 per cent of women. The gender gap is still closing.

Email is the most intensively used service, followed by information searches, checking news, taking courses, doing job-related tasks, shopping and paying bills, searching for jobs, and games or entertainment.

TOP INTERNET USERS
end 2000

- Germany 5%
- UK 5%
- China 4%
- Canada 4%
- Japan 7%
- South Korea 4%
- Italy 3%
- Brazil 3%
- France 2%
- Australia 2%
- USA 36%
- rest of world 24%

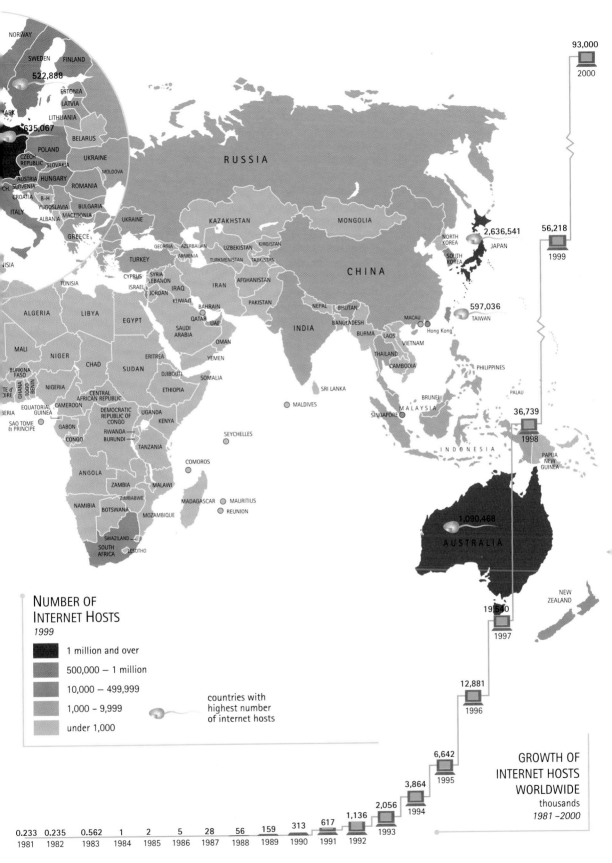

NORWAY
SWEDEN FINLAND
522,888
ESTONIA
LATVIA
LITHUANIA
ARK
635,067
BELARUS
POLAND
CZECH
REPUBLIC SLOVAKIA
CH. SLOVENIA HUNGARY
CROATIA ROMANIA
AUSTRIA
B-H
ITALY YUGOSLAVIA BULGARIA
ALBANIA MACEDONIA
GREECE
UKRAINE
MOLDOVA

NISIA
TUNISIA

RUSSIA

KAZAKHSTAN

MONGOLIA

GEORGIA AZERBAIJAN
ARMENIA UZBEKISTAN KIRGISTAN
TURKMENISTAN TAJIKISTAN

NORTH
KOREA
2,636,541
JAPAN
SOUTH
KOREA

CYPRUS SYRIA
ISRAEL LEBANON
JORDAN IRAQ
KUWAIT
BAHRAIN
QATAR
UAE
OMAN
YEMEN

TURKEY

CHINA

IRAN
AFGHANISTAN
PAKISTAN

NEPAL BHUTAN
BANGLADESH
INDIA
BURMA

MACAU
Hong Kong

597,036
TAIWAN

ALGERIA LIBYA EGYPT
SAUDI
ARABIA

LAOS
THAILAND VIETNAM
CAMBODIA

PHILIPPINES

PALAU

MALI
NIGER CHAD SUDAN ERITREA
BURKINA
FASO DJIBOUTI
NIGERIA SOMALIA
GHANA
TE d' BENIN CENTRAL ETHIOPIA
OIRE TOGO AFRICAN REPUBLIC
BERIA CAMEROON
EQUATORIAL
SAO TOME GUINEA DEMOCRATIC UGANDA
& PRINCIPE GABON REPUBLIC OF KENYA
CONGO CONGO
RWANDA
BURUNDI
TANZANIA

SRI LANKA

MALDIVES

BRUNEI
MALAYSIA
SINGAPORE

INDONESIA

36,739
1998

PAPUA
NEW
GUINEA

SEYCHELLES

ANGOLA
ZAMBIA MALAWI
NAMIBIA ZIMBABWE
BOTSWANA MOZAMBIQUE
SWAZILAND
SOUTH LESOTHO
AFRICA

COMOROS

MADAGASCAR MAURITIUS
REUNION

1,090,468
AUSTRALIA

NEW
ZEALAND

19,540
1997

NUMBER OF INTERNET HOSTS
1999

◼	1 million and over
◼	500,000 – 1 million
◼	10,000 – 499,999
◼	1,000 – 9,999
◼	under 1,000

countries with
highest number
of internet hosts

12,881
1996

6,642
1995

3,864
1994

GROWTH OF INTERNET HOSTS WORLDWIDE
thousands
1981 –2000

2,056
1993

1,136
1992

0.233	0.235	0.562	1	2	5	28	56	159	313	617
1981	1982	1983	1984	1985	1986	1987	1988	1989	1990	1991

INTERNET REGULATION

Here are three myths of our time. The Internet is not regulated. The Internet cannot be regulated. The Internet should not be regulated.

In fact, the Internet always has been regulated. For the first 15 years of its existence funding from the US government and military made the Internet possible, and they called the shots. Since the early 1990s, an informal regime of commercial regulation has emerged. To gain access to the Internet, we have to subscribe to Internet Service Providers (ISPs) such as America Online or Compuserve. Then, to track down a specific site, we use search engines such as Excite, Infoseek, Lycos or Yahoo. These service providers and search engine companies play an increasingly powerful role in determining what information is available, and the paths by which we can reach it. It is no surprise to find major entertainment, software, and telecommunications companies buying into the field, with Disney acquiring Infoseek for $473 million in June 1998 (see *Disney* page 65) and At Home Network, a high-speed Internet service for cable television subscribers, acquiring Excite Inc for $6 billion in January 1999.

The regulation of these *de facto* regulators will, primarily, be national governments and national courts – although international bodies such as the UN's World Intellectual Property Organization (WIPO) are beginning to have some impact too. (Net police squads have been formed in Germany, France, Canada, Italy, UK, USA, Japan and Russia.) National powers may be limited, however. The sender of the Love Bug virus that caused millions of dollars worth of damage around the world in 2000 could not be prosecuted under existing Philippines law. It is also true, as the information on the map shows, that some governments use the pretext of protecting citizens from "subversive ideas" or defending "national security and unity" to deny access to the Internet, usually by forcing them to subscribe to a state-run ISP. Nevertheless, there are certain types of conduct that are properly regarded as being unacceptable on the Internet as they are elsewhere.

The argument is not really about whether or not the Internet is regulated. It is. The question is, who does the regulating – private, mostly US-owned companies or national governments and international organizations – and where should the limits of acceptable conduct be drawn? Libertarians express outrage at such events as the French courts convicting Yahoo for allowing a site promoting the sale of Nazi memorabilia, for example. There are starkly opposing views about the legitimacy (and the legality) of downloading copyright material from the Web (see *World Music* pages 90-91). There have been some areas, however, in which there has been concerted international action to control conduct on the Internet without too much controversy. In May 2000, the FBI and the National White Collar Crime Center in the USA set up the Internet Fraud Complaint Center (IFCC) to counter Internet fraud globally (see below). A specialist squad in New Zealand arrested 250 people using the Internet to access or distribute child pornography between 1999 and 2000.

Internet regulation creates interesting dilemmas for states such as Malaysia and Singapore, where the inclination is to limit public access to information for the supposedly greater good of social cohesion. This moral authoritarianism runs into conflict with the economic advantages to be gained from online trade and access to technical and scientific information. So far, the economic argument seems to be winning out. It is also interesting to compare the actual level of convictions for Internet-related offences in states with a free press and those with a censored press. In Germany, for example, there are about 1,000 convictions per year, primarily for anti-Semitism and pornography. In the USA, convictions have averaged about 400 per year since 1996. By contrast, in China, for all its formal restrictions on press freedom, there have been no more than 400 convictions in total since 1995. In Singapore there have been fewer than ten.

MAJOR TYPES OF INTERNET FRAUD

As reported to the IFFC *2000*

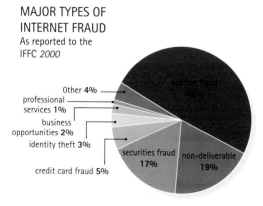

Other 4%
professional services 1%
business opportunities 2%
identity theft 3%
credit card fraud 5%
securities fraud 17%
non-deliverable 19%

STATE RESTRAINTS ON INTERNET ACCESS

Selected countries *2000*

Uzbekistan and Azerbaijan
The operations of privately owned ISPs are tightly controlled by telecommunications ministries, which also clamp down on any criticism of the government.

China
In October 1998, the Chinese authorities blocked access to the BBC website. In January 1999, a computer technician in Shanghai, Lin Hai, was sentenced to two years in prison for passing the email addresses of 30,000 Chinese subscribers to the publishers of a US-based dissident online magazine. As the tenth anniversary of the Tiananmen massacre approached on 4 June 1999, anxious officials ordered the closure of 300 cyber cafés in Shanghai on the grounds that they lacked the correct authorization.

North Korea
Prior to 2000, access to the Internet was impossible from Pyongyang. The national news agency and some newspapers and ministries maintain official websites aimed at foreigners through servers located in Japan.

Belarus
Government allows Internet access only through a single state-owned ISP, Belpak.

Iran
Sexuality, religion, criticism of the Islamic Republic, any mention of Israel or the USA – all are censored on the Internet as in other media. Access to many sites is banned. Even medical students in Iran are denied access to Internet pages dealing with human anatomy.

Syria
Individual Syrian citizens are officially barred from access to the Internet, and face the penalty of a possible prison sentence. The public telecommunications authority's ISP maintains websites for the national news agency, state newspapers and a few ministries.

Kazakhstan and Kirgistan
Governments charge ISPs prohibitively expensive usage and connection fees.

Tajikistan
Access is only possible at all in Dushanbe, where it is controlled by a single government-owned ISP, Telecom Technologies.

Libya
Citizens are not able to access or explore the Internet.

Turkmenistan
Access is severely restricted.

Cuba
About ten illegal news agencies, such as Cubanet and Cuba Free Press, telephone reports to Miami-based émigrés, who then publish them on the Internet.

Sudan
The Sudanese state controls the few possible connections to the Internet through its monopoly ISP, Sudanet.

Iraq
The West's post-Gulf War sanctions against Iraq mean that very few people own computers. Even those who do own one have no direct access to the Internet. The official Iraqi press and some ministries maintain websites through servers based in Jordan.

Burma
The state holds a monopoly on Internet access, and imposes total censorship. Failure to declare ownership of a computer to the government renders an individual liable to a 15-year prison sentence.

Tunisia
The Tunisian Internet Agency (ATI) controls two privately owned ISPs – one owned by President Ben Ali's daughter and the other by a presidential crony. In 1998, responding to an Amnesty International report condemning human rights violations in Tunisia, a public relations company closely linked to the government published a website with the deliberately confusing address www.amnesty-tunisia.org. It praised the president's work for human rights fulsomely. Meanwhile, access to Amnesty International's official site was blocked.

Sierra Leone
In June 1999, two journalists from the daily *Independent Observer* were arrested and accused of collaborating with the online newspaper *Ninjas* being produced outside Sierra Leone by journalists who had fled the country.

Saudi Arabia
The Internet is officially condemned in Saudi Arabia as "a harmful force for Westernizing people's minds". Even so, 37 private ISPs have been licensed to operate, subject to all traffic being routed through the servers of the Science and Technology Centre. This centre is equipped with filters banning access to sites that provide "information contrary to Islamic values".

Vietnam
Vietnamese citizens seeking Internet access require permission from the interior ministry, and have to sign up with one of the two state-owned ISPs. These ISPs block access to sites maintained by international human rights organizations and by Vietnamese organizations based abroad.

ELECTRONIC MAIL

Faxes, emails and short messages transmitted by cell phone are all examples of electronic "small media" – methods by which people communicate with a specialized, self-defined network. As the technology develops, the boundaries between different methods of communication begin to blur.

Small media are often associated with democratic movements and protest, and can include everything from the mobilization of anti-globalization protestors to Vietnamese women communicating with other women's groups throughout the world. The rapid mobilization of hundreds of thousands of anti-Estrada demonstrators in the Philippines in January 2001 was almost certainly brought about by the use of short messaging.

Fax and emailing technologies, together with personal computers, have replaced the office typewriter. By mid-1995 Smith-Corona, while still selling over 70 percent of typewriters in the USA, had filed for bankruptcy. These technologies have not created the predicted "paperless office", however. Businesses that become computer and IT intensive actually increase their paper consumption by up to 50 percent.

Webmail services, which provide a free mailbox in exchange for advertising on every page sent, are increasingly popular. By the end of 1999 there were nearly 170 million Webmail accounts, double the number for the previous year and more than eight times as many as in 1997. Hotmail and Yahoo! remained the leaders. The linking of advertising to "free services" can now be seen in a range of media, from telecommunications to traditional media.

The ability of online mail and other electronic services to allow organizations to construct personal profiles of their users raises issues of privacy, and the difficulty of regulating the use of email leads to other concerns (see opposite). Email allows people to abuse others on a scale never previously imagined. In 2000, the virus-monitoring company MessageLabs detected and stopped about 155,528 email viruses up to the end of November 2000 – about one every 3 minutes. In October 2000 alone the company detected 30,678 viruses.

USA 2000
Nearly two-thirds of employees used email and a quarter of all households had at least one electronic mailbox.

IRELAND
UNITED KINGDOM
BELGIUM
FRANCE
PORTUGAL
SPAIN
MOROCCO
ALGERIA
GAMBIA
GUINEA
BISSAU
GUINEA
SIERRA

CANADA

UNITED STATES OF AMERICA

MEXICO

DOMINICAN REPUBLIC

COSTA RICA
VENEZUELA
TRINIDAD & TOBAGO
COLOMBIA

BRAZIL

CHILE

ARGENTINA

MAILBOX GROWTH
Number of electronic mailboxes worldwide
1990–1999
millions

569

15

1990 1999

MAILBOX DISTRIBUTION
Mailbox registration
1999

rest of world
236 million

USA
333 million

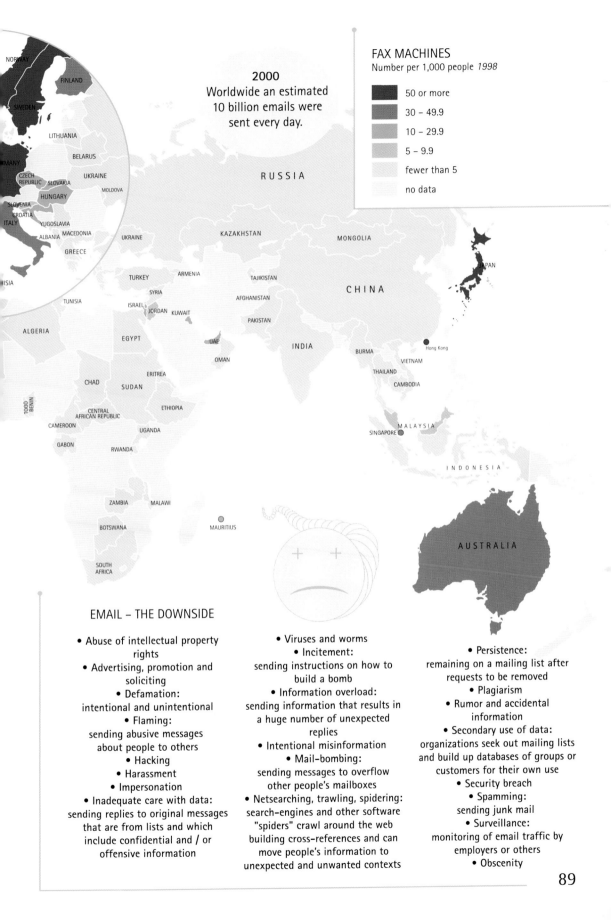

2000
Worldwide an estimated
10 billion emails were
sent every day.

NORWAY, FINLAND, SWEDEN, LITHUANIA, GERMANY, BELARUS, CZECH REPUBLIC, SLOVAKIA, UKRAINE, SLOVENIA, HUNGARY, MOLDOVA, CROATIA, ITALY, YUGOSLAVIA, ALBANIA, MACEDONIA, GREECE

RUSSIA

KAZAKHSTAN, MONGOLIA

UKRAINE, TURKEY, ARMENIA, TAJIKISTAN, CHINA, JAPAN

SYRIA, AFGHANISTAN, TUNISIA, ISRAEL, JORDAN, KUWAIT

ALGERIA, EGYPT, PAKISTAN, UAE, INDIA, BURMA, Hong Kong, OMAN, VIETNAM

CHAD, ERITREA, THAILAND, CAMBODIA, SUDAN, TOGO, BENIN, CENTRAL AFRICAN REPUBLIC, ETHIOPIA, CAMEROON, UGANDA, MALAYSIA, SINGAPORE, GABON, RWANDA

INDONESIA

ZAMBIA, MALAWI, MAURITIUS

BOTSWANA, AUSTRALIA

SOUTH AFRICA

EMAIL – THE DOWNSIDE

- Abuse of intellectual property rights
- Advertising, promotion and soliciting
- Defamation: intentional and unintentional
- Flaming: sending abusive messages about people to others
- Hacking
- Harassment
- Impersonation
- Inadequate care with data: sending replies to original messages that are from lists and which include confidential and / or offensive information

- Viruses and worms
- Incitement: sending instructions on how to build a bomb
- Information overload: sending information that results in a huge number of unexpected replies
- Intentional misinformation
- Mail-bombing: sending messages to overflow other people's mailboxes
- Netsearching, trawling, spidering: search-engines and other software "spiders" crawl around the web building cross-references and can move people's information to unexpected and unwanted contexts

- Persistence: remaining on a mailing list after requests to be removed
- Plagiarism
- Rumor and accidental information
- Secondary use of data: organizations seek out mailing lists and build up databases of groups or customers for their own use
- Security breach
- Spamming: sending junk mail
- Surveillance: monitoring of email traffic by employers or others
- Obscenity

89

WEBSITES

Although the Internet was first developed in the 1970s, the World Wide Web was not launched until 1991. Its aim – providing a means by which individuals could access and use the Internet – had a huge impact on public consciousness, and this expectation of public accessibility informed the definition of the Internet drawn up by the Federal Networking Council (FNC) in 1995 (see *Glossary* page 118).

Estimates of the total size of the Web vary from 22 million to over 800 million sites, depending on what is being counted. Some pages are indexed through search engines. Others, such as those holding university course materials, business

directories and subscription sites, restrict access and may not be indexed. Some indexed sites are simply home pages behind which lie hundreds of pages of documents. What is clear is that there is an extraordinary amount of information out there, which is being added to daily as the wired world – and in particular the commercial world – wholeheartedly embraces the Web ("What's on Websites").

Most people find their way through the Web by means of search engines such as Alta Vista, Google and Yahoo (which, although relatively small, remains popular). Each of the search engines indexes millions of web pages, the precise number being difficult to establish (see "Search engines" opposite). The indexes overlap to a large extent, but some search engines find pages that others miss. In 2000 a study ran five identical searches were through 14 search engines. Although 795 "hits" were made, this amounted to only 298 different webpages. On the other hand, 110 of these webpages were only found by one search engines, of which 40 were found by Fast. The proportion of the Web that is indexed by the

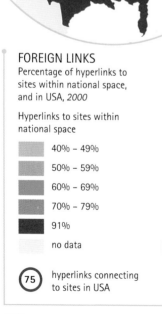

FOREIGN LINKS

Percentage of hyperlinks to sites within national space, and in USA, *2000*

Hyperlinks to sites within national space

- 40% – 49%
- 50% – 59%
- 60% – 69%
- 70% – 79%
- 91%
- no data

(75) hyperlinks connecting to sites in USA

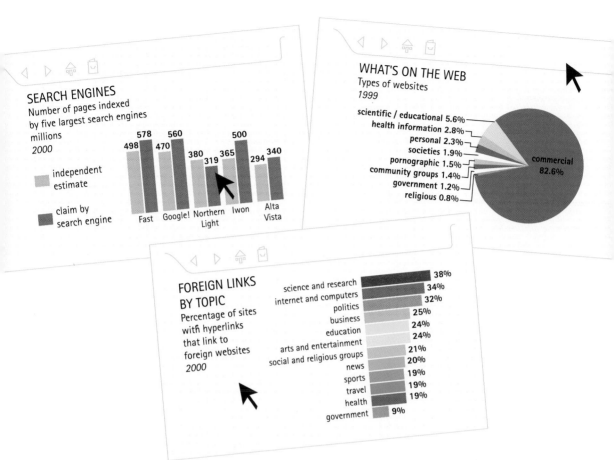

SEARCH ENGINES
Number of pages indexed by five largest search engines
millions
2000

- independent estimate
- claim by search engine

	Fast	Google!	Northern Light	Iwon	Alta Vista
independent	498	470	380 / 319	365	294
claim	578	560		500	340

WHAT'S ON THE WEB
Types of websites
1999

- scientific / educational 5.6%
- health information 2.8%
- personal 2.3%
- societies 1.9%
- pornographic 1.5%
- community groups 1.4%
- government 1.2%
- religious 0.8%
- commercial 82.6%

FOREIGN LINKS BY TOPIC
Percentage of sites with hyperlinks that link to foreign websites
2000

Topic	%
science and research	38%
internet and computers	34%
politics	32%
business	25%
education	24%
arts and entertainment	24%
social and religious groups	21%
news	20%
sports	19%
travel	19%
health	19%
government	9%

search engines is hotly contested, but it is probably fewer than half of all the sites.

Domain names – the electronic addresses of businesses, organizations and individuals – are proliferating at a remarkable rate, as companies, organizations and individuals rush to register their own unique Internet address. They are competing against "cybersquatters" – people who register any domain name they perceive as potentially advantageous. Some attempt to sell a name to the highest bidder, others use a name to damage a company or organization with the same name – perhaps by masquerading as that company on the Web, or by misdirecting genuine enquiries. The rights of the cybersquatter are being challenged and undermined, as disputes over ownership of domain names reach the courts.

Most countries have adopted a coding system that identifies a domain's nationality (.fr for France or .de for Germany, for example). The USA, as inventor of the system, is the exception. Some

countries, such as the UK and Australia, have established a further level of coding to indicate the type of domain – .ac for academic, .org for organization and .com for company. Domain registration data shows that English-speaking and industrialized nations are well ahead of countries whose telecommunications are underdeveloped. However, some smaller states, and certain geographically isolated locations, are wholeheartedly embracing the Web as a simple and cheap way of, for example, providing tourist information.

The fact that domain names are still largely classified in terms of national boundaries is ironic, given the Web's global ideal. An examination of the extent to which websites make links across borders reveals a mixed picture, in which language barriers still hold sway ("Foreign links by topic" above). When the websites are broken down by topic some areas, such as academic research, are shown to be more international in outlook than others (see above).

Global Village, Global Market

8

In 2001, the US movie title *Men in Black* (MIB) was adopted
by a Taiwanese band, *Music is Back* (MIB). They made
a music video in which three middle-aged men,
dressed in Star Wars costumes and Raybans,
sang Taiwanese folksongs
of the 1970s and 1980s.

E-Tourism

The growth of business transactions over the Internet has had an impact on the way people buy and sell goods, the way they interact with other people, and their experience (or otherwise) of the consumer cultures in which they live. There are also specific trends in e-tailing that raise interesting questions about the way we experience the world. E-tourism is the current term to describe one such phenomenon. As the tourism industry has boomed (see below), predictions have been made about the healthy attendant growth of e-travel, e-ticketing and e-planning (see opposite).

before making a booking people are able to get the most out of what may be very limited vacation periods (see "Average number of vacation days" below).

There is more to e-tourism than simple convenience, however. As the equivalent of the holiday brochure goes online it takes on special

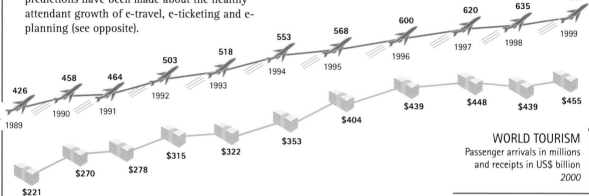

WORLD TOURISM
Passenger arrivals in millions and receipts in US$ billion
2000

Year	Arrivals	Receipts
1989	426	$221
1990	458	$270
1991	464	$278
1992	503	$315
1993	518	$322
1994	553	$353
1995	568	$404
1996	600	$439
1997	620	$448
1998	635	$439
1999	657	$455

More and more people in the developed world have the money to travel overseas. Although many still prefer the safety of a package holiday, others are willing to leave the security of their group and venture beyond the pre-arranged familiarity of their material and cultural habits. A significant proportion of this group of more adventurous travellers (in particular those from the USA) are using the Internet to find and book the experience they seek. It is much more pleasant to go online at home than to stand in line at a travel agent and wait while they go online for you. And by researching a destination online

qualities. It can be enhanced with sound and animation. It can offer virtual visits to key historic and cultural sites. It can preview the delights and the selected highlights of a chosen destination. This can be fun for the browser, but it may also further predetermine the type of experience the physical traveller may have once they are "somewhere else". In some cases, this adventure is a prequel, in others it may substitute for actual travel – the homebody can travel virtually, without expenditure, and with no fear of change and cultural insecurity.

USA 2003
Revenue from e-tourism expected to reach between 10% and 23% of total tourism revenue.

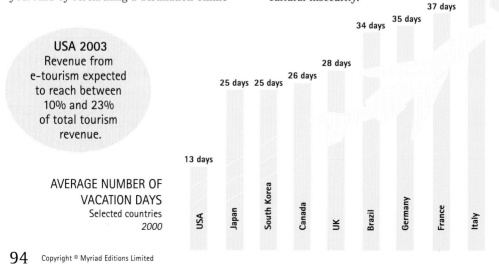

AVERAGE NUMBER OF VACATION DAYS
Selected countries
2000

USA	13 days
Japan	25 days
South Korea	25 days
Canada	26 days
UK	28 days
Brazil	34 days
Germany	35 days
France	37 days
Italy	42 days

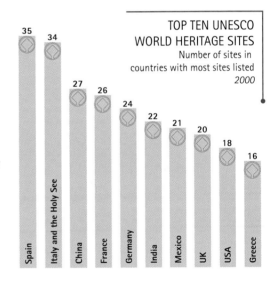

PROJECTED INCREASE IN
E-TRAVEL BY EUROPEANS
US$ billion
1997–2003 projected

$23.4
2003

$20.6
2002

$16.3
2001

$10.4
2000

$6
1999

$2.5
1998

$0.6
1997

Such websites are also important for regions seeking to enhance their global profile, or to correct misconceptions. For this reason Unesco has funded a program to locate and promote some of the top websites relating to events and places in Africa. These include sites on festivals of poetry, contemporary African music and art.

Another form of enhanced substitution is the online museum or art gallery. The Museums Online Network alone lists over 1,000 museums that have an Internet presence. These sites are designed as advertisements for the museums themselves and to give information to potential visitors. Unfortunately, although 85 percent of online visitors are seeking images of artefacts and artworks housed in the museums and galleries, these are available only on the more sophisticated websites (see below). Of course, this kind of experience is unmodified by face-to-face engagement, difficulties and random conversations. It becomes easy – perhaps too easy – to think that one "knows" about another place, or about different ways of living. By the same token, however, individual pieces of art become visible and, in the best-designed virtual spaces, almost tangible. If the digital divide were not so great, the cultural memories of the world potentially could become open to all, regardless of their ability to travel. Given that more than half of virtual

visitors find online museums by chance, it also seems that the virtual wanderer finds culture that they might not otherwise encounter.

Finally, there is institutionalized heritage. There are 690 sites listed by Unesco's World Heritage Committee: 529 cultural sites, 138 natural sites, and 23 mixed. These sites are spread across 122 different countries, but of the ten states with the highest number of sites, six are from Europe (see below). Although sacred and historic sites important to Asian, South American and African cultures are listed, the majority of the sites reinforce Western concepts of cultural importance. Although places of natural beauty in Australia are often also of sacred importance to indigenous peoples, the environmental aspect tends to be privileged over the sacred imperative in world heritage descriptions.

TOP TEN UNESCO
WORLD HERITAGE SITES
Number of sites in
countries with most sites listed
2000

Spain	Italy and the Holy See	China	France	Germany	India	Mexico	UK	USA	Greece
35	34	27	26	24	22	21	20	18	16

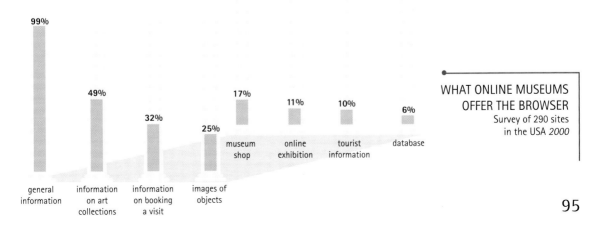

WHAT ONLINE MUSEUMS
OFFER THE BROWSER
Survey of 290 sites
in the USA *2000*

general information	information on art collections	information on booking a visit	images of objects	museum shop	online exhibition	tourist information	database
99%	49%	32%	25%	17%	11%	10%	6%

WORLD MUSIC

Recorded music is common across the media spectrum. Radio stations rely on it for their audience share, television companies organize youth programming around it, and live music and entertainment venues depend on it as a commercial context for their operation. Most of all, however, it is the artists themselves and the record companies, who need recorded music technologies in order to survive.

These technologies have changed rapidly with the arrival of digital media. Music is sold on CD, mini and maxi disk, and, increasingly, is available on the Internet in mp3 files (see "Top Music Sites" below). The possibility of free downloads of music is the key issue in music media news at present, and will continue to be so until international copyright law catches up with the possibilities and realities of digitally compressed music files. Whilst record companies fear losses in revenue from the sites that offer downloads and music sharing from pier to pier, many artists argue that the exposure that these networks afford their work is beneficial to world music and commercial diversity. The likely compromise seems to be the subscription site, where networks and producing companies charge rates for the number of plays on real audio.

The music scene beyond the Internet is still huge, however. Sales of music continue to be largest in the USA, Japan and the UK, although the market profiles of these countries are quite different. Sales of singles are relatively insignificant in the USA (see opposite), whereas they comprise more than a third of the Japanese market.

Despite the globalization of the music market, there is continuing loyalty world wide to "local repertoire", which comprises 66 percent of recorded music purchases. That said, there are some interesting hybrid tastes. Cantopop and Ethnic pop are important genres in Asia and in Latin America respectively, but Western Classical music features significantly in South Korea and German-speaking countries.

Despite the availability of many formats, people's choice relies on the cost of the hardware that supports the new packages. In the USA 1997 was the crossover year from cassette singles and maxi-singles to CD singles. These sales were boosted by the affordability of CD boom-boxes

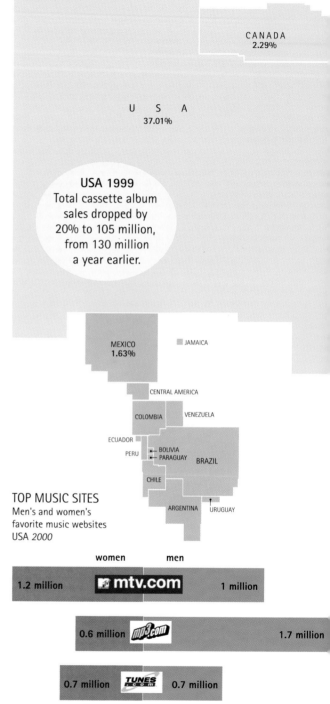

CANADA
2.29%

U S A
37.01%

USA 1999
Total cassette album sales dropped by 20% to 105 million, from 130 million a year earlier.

MEXICO
1.63%

JAMAICA

CENTRAL AMERICA

COLOMBIA

VENEZUELA

ECUADOR

PERU

BOLIVIA

PARAGUAY

BRAZIL

CHILE

ARGENTINA

URUGUAY

TOP MUSIC SITES
Men's and women's favorite music websites
USA 2000

women   men

| 1.2 million | mtv.com | 1 million |

| 0.6 million | mp3.com | 1.7 million |

| 0.7 million | TUNES | 0.7 million |

and walkman-CDs. It appears that the technology must match the ways in which music is consumed in mobile urban environments – on the run.

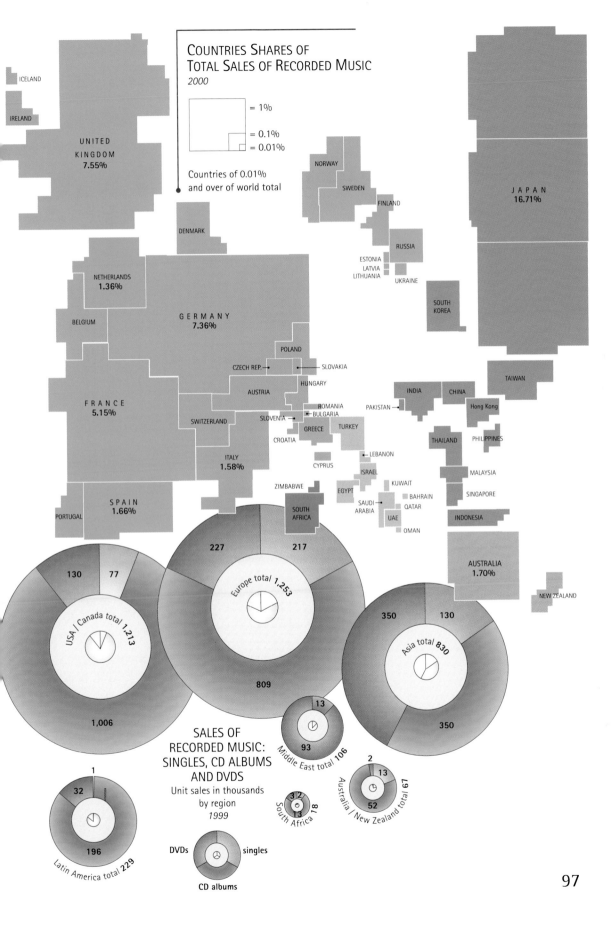

COUNTRIES SHARES OF
TOTAL SALES OF RECORDED MUSIC
2000

= 1%
= 0.1%
= 0.01%

Countries of 0.01%
and over of world total

ICELAND

IRELAND

UNITED
KINGDOM
7.55%

NORWAY

SWEDEN

FINLAND

JAPAN
16.71%

DENMARK

RUSSIA

ESTONIA
LATVIA
LITHUANIA

UKRAINE

NETHERLANDS
1.36%

BELGIUM

GERMANY
7.36%

POLAND

CZECH REP. — SLOVAKIA

HUNGARY

AUSTRIA

ROMANIA

SLOVENIA — BULGARIA

SWITZERLAND

GREECE

TURKEY

CROATIA

ITALY
1.58%

CYPRUS

LEBANON

ISRAEL

KUWAIT

BAHRAIN

ZIMBABWE

EGYPT

SAUDI
ARABIA

QATAR

SOUTH
AFRICA

UAE

OMAN

SPAIN
1.66%

PORTUGAL

SOUTH
KOREA

TAIWAN

INDIA

CHINA

Hong Kong

PAKISTAN

THAILAND

PHILIPPINES

MALAYSIA

SINGAPORE

INDONESIA

AUSTRALIA
1.70%

NEW ZEALAND

FRANCE
5.15%

130   77

USA / Canada total 1,213

1,006

227   217

Europe total 1,253

809

350   130

Asia total 830

350

13

Middle East total 106

93

SALES OF
RECORDED MUSIC:
SINGLES, CD ALBUMS
AND DVDS
Unit sales in thousands
by region
1999

3 2
13
South Africa 18

2
13
Australia / New Zealand total 67
52

1

32

196

Latin America total 229

DVDs   singles

CD albums

97

WOMEN AND MEDIA

In 1995 the UN Conference on Women in Beijing resolved to improve women's position in the media industries and to encourage a more balanced presentation of women in the media. At the beginning of the 21st century, however, inequalities of access, control of production and presentation remain.

Women in many parts of the world are poorly catered for by the print media, with hardly any titles in Africa and the Middle East addressing women's interests and issues. By contrast, in the USA, Europe and Southeast Asia, women are well provided with specialist magazines (see map). This is because they are considered as valuable advertising targets. Their "desirability" is also demonstrated by the fact that television advertising aimed at the "TV Housewife" (an industry term referring to the main grocery shopper) has considerably more money spent on it than advertising aimed at adults in general (see inset map).

Women's access to the Internet varies around the world (see below). In some countries they have equal access, and take advantage of it; in others they either do not have access, or feel unable or unwilling to use it for cultural reasons. Many women in African and Middle Eastern countries lack the higher education that would give them the confidence to use the Internet, and older women in particular may lack the literacy skills.

Women who do use the Internet tend to access shopping sites, kids' sites and sites with the word "women" in the address. They may also use it to safeguard their anonymity when venturing into traditionally male-dominated areas, such as online dating, sex and gambling. Twenty-two percent of women surveyed in the UK about their gambling habits said that the Internet provided a safe, fun, *anonymous* way to gamble.

Increasingly, the trend is for both the content and delivery of media aimed at women to converge. The highly successful "Oprah" brand name ties television show, magazine and online site together, and her "recommended books" invariably make it onto the international bestseller lists.

The representation of women in the media has been the subject of detailed study in the industrialized world. Statistics from the USA show that women represent only 40 percent of characters in prime-time television drama (this proportion sinking to 36 percent for workplace sitcoms). Younger women predominate, with only 16 percent of female characters being over 40 years old. This is probably partly because only around 23 percent of creative workers in US television companies are women – very few of whom are directors of photography.

CANADA

UNITED STATES OF AMERICA

DOMINICAN REPUBLIC

PUERTO RICO

GUATEMALA

COSTA RICA

VENEZUELA

BRA

CHILE

ARGENTINA

8 hours
6 hours
5 hours
3 hours
7 hours
5 hours
9 hours
6 hours
6 hours
4 hours
10 hours
8 hours

55%   55%   58%   52%   61%   49%   51%
       45%   45%   42%   48%   39%

WOMEN AS INTERNET USERS
Hours per month of Internet use and percentages of men and women users
2000 selected countries

men
women

Australia   Ireland   Singapore   New Zealand   UK   USA

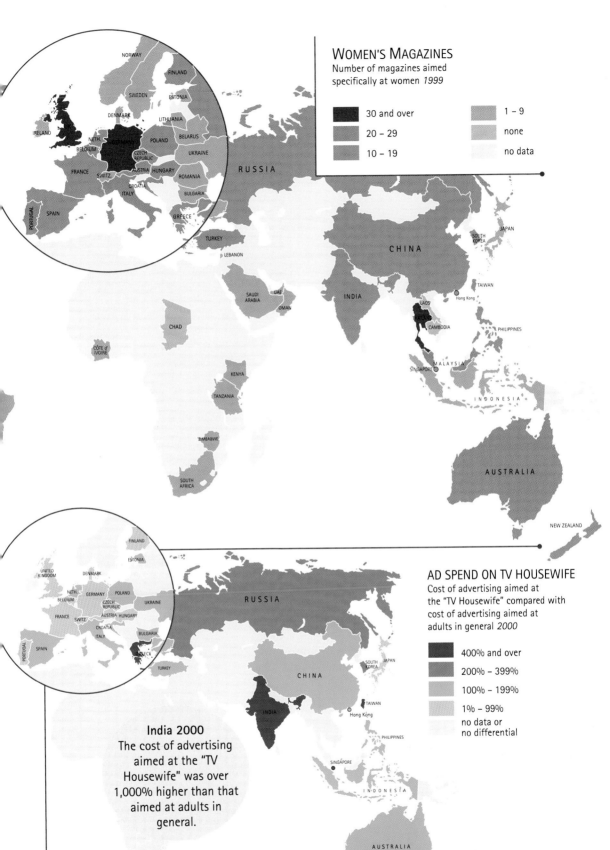

WOMEN'S MAGAZINES
Number of magazines aimed specifically at women *1999*

- 30 and over
- 20 – 29
- 10 – 19
- 1 – 9
- none
- no data

AD SPEND ON TV HOUSEWIFE
Cost of advertising aimed at the "TV Housewife" compared with cost of advertising aimed at adults in general *2000*

- 400% and over
- 200% – 399%
- 100% – 199%
- 1% – 99%
- no data or no differential

India 2000
The cost of advertising aimed at the "TV Housewife" was over 1,000% higher than that aimed at adults in general.

99

Over one third of the world's population is under 18 years old. Many live in the least developed countries, beyond the reach of most types of media, but around 2 billion children in industrialized and industrializing countries are targeted by huge media corporations. The big four players in this particular playground are Fox Family Worldwide, Nickelodeon, Time Warner and Walt Disney.

In 1999, broadcasters spent over US$2 billion on producing, commissioning and acquiring children's programs. Between them, the USA, Japan, the UK, France and Germany absorb 80 percent of spending on children's broadcast material, with 40 percent of programs being produced in the USA, 33 percent in Western Europe and 22 percent in Asia.

Disney, above all, is the studio that has perfected the art of the child audience. It has targeted children not just as movie and television consumers, but also as the objects of sophisticated marketing tie-ins between the cartoons and associated merchandizing. In 1929 Disney allowed Mickey Mouse to be reproduced on school slates. A year later Mickey Mouse dolls went into production and throughout the 1930s the Mickey brand name and image were licensed with huge success. In 1955 *The Mickey Mouse Club* was aired on US network television. By then the economic logic of the children's media market was firmly in place. The toys promote the films,

and Disney is happy. Films, television and now home videos promote the toys, and the toy-makers are happy. The theme parks – Disneyland and Disneyworld – promote the characters and the equation between Disney and childhood, and everyone is happy – except perhaps the out-of-pocket parents. Disney is currently the world's second largest media conglomerate, after AOL Time Warner, with sales of US$23.4 billion in 1999. It generates nearly a third of its revenue from broadcasting, 26 percent from theme parks, and the rest from "creative content" – films, home videos and DVDs, books and comics, computer games, merchandising, and the goldmine that is the Disney archive (see *Disney* pages 64–65).

The marketing juggernaut makes people nervous. Parents want to feel confident that television – sometimes known as the Electronic Babysitter – is promoting virtues (see below), while there are plenty of people who are only too happy to tell them that television is destroying their children's physical and spiritual health. The jury is still out over whether children are innocent and vulnerable victims or media-savvy consumers. Often the media are blamed for intractable social failures – poverty, racism, unemployment, inadequate education, family violence – and much of the so-called evidence about media effects is produced to back up that entrenched political position. Psychological tests claiming to show that only the media are responsible for violence among children should be treated with scepticism.

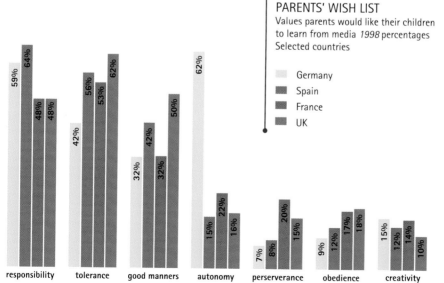

PARENTS' WISH LIST
Values parents would like their children to learn from media *1998* percentages
Selected countries

Germany
Spain
France
UK

responsibility: 59% 64% 48% 48%
tolerance: 42% 56% 53% 62%
good manners: 32% 42% 32% 50%
autonomy: 62% 15% 22% 16%
perserverance: 7% 8% 20% 15%
obedience: 9% 12% 17% 18%
creativity: 15% 12% 14% 10%

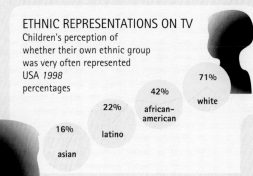

ETHNIC REPRESENTATIONS ON TV

Children's perception of
whether their own ethnic group
was very often represented
USA *1998*
percentages

71% white

42% african-american

22% latino

16% asian

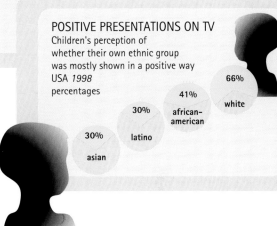

POSITIVE PRESENTATIONS ON TV

Children's perception of
whether their own ethnic group
was mostly shown in a positive way
USA *1998*
percentages

66% white

41% african-american

30% latino

30% asian

More interesting, though less conclusive, is research into how children make sense of media messages. A 1998 survey in the USA, for example, suggests that age is the most reliable guide to tastes among 10- to 17-year-olds. There are also demographic differences, however, and some likely cultural explanations for them. If a noticeably larger proportion of white teenagers in the USA tune in to sitcoms, could it be because they feature so many young white people, and show them in a positive light? Many African-American teenagers feel that they are represented in a less than positive way, when at all, on television (see above), which may explain why they prefer to watch music videos.

The prevalence and popularity of foreign-produced programs and the absence of local content is always a vexed issue (see below). Will children pick up bad habits? Will they fail to absorb traditional local values? How will children "read" foreign content? Again, it may be a mistake to focus too much on behavioral or attitudinal influences. Television programs for children should be judged in terms of quality and values, not in terms of largely unpredictable consequences for individual viewers or groups of viewers. Children deserve high-quality media, not books, films, programs or websites that are dishonestly sentimental, exploitative, racist, grossly violent or simply tacky.

In Fiji television was not introduced until 1995. A survey found that after watching foreign shows like *Xena: Warrior Princess, ER, Seinfeld,* and *Melrose Place* 74% of a sample of teenage girls felt that they were "too fat".

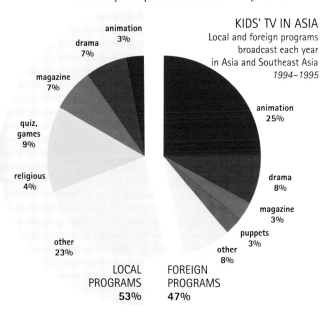

KIDS' TV IN ASIA
Local and foreign programs broadcast each year in Asia and Southeast Asia *1994–1995*

animation 3%

drama 7%

magazine 7%

quiz, games 9%

religious 4%

other 23%

animation 25%

drama 8%

magazine 3%

puppets 3%

other 8%

LOCAL PROGRAMS 53%

FOREIGN PROGRAMS 47%

WORLD TABLE

Countries	1 POPULATION thousands 1999	2 POPULATION Under 5 years old thousands 1999	3 POPULATION Under 18 years old thousands 1999	4 POPULATION GROWTH projected annual rate 1998-2015	5 ADULT MALE LITERACY percentages 1999
Afghanistan	21,923	4,190	10,740	–	46
Albania	3,113	305	1,102	1.0	–
Algeria	30,774	4,085	13,530	1.7	73
Angola	12,479	2,389	6,749	2.8	56
Argentina	36,577	3,483	12,199	1.0	97
Armenia	3,525	232	1,101	0.4	100
Australia	18,705	1,259	4,687	0.8	–
Austria	8,177	434	1,705	−0.1	–
Azerbaijan	7,697	639	2,717	0.9	99
Bahamas	301	33	108	–	95
Bahrain	606	61	214	–	87
Bangladesh	126,947	15,120	55,733	1.5	63
Barbados	269	17	71	–	98
Belarus	10,274	505	2,479	−0.5	100
Belgium	10,152	549	2,114	0.0	–
Belize	235	34	111	–	75
Benin	5,937	1,033	3,175	2.5	43
Bhutan	2,064	339	1,009	–	56
Bolivia	8,142	1,200	3,763	1.9	92
Bosnia-Herzegovina	3,839	198	926	0.8	98
Botswana	1,597	241	794	0.9	70
Brazil	167,988	15,993	59,861	1.1	86
Brunei	322	35	124	–	93
Bulgaria	8,279	368	1,723	−0.7	99
Burkina Faso	11,616	2,185	6,295	2.3	29
Burma	45,059	4,226	15,844	1.1	88
Burundi	6,565	1,154	3,502	2.0	48
Cambodia	10,945	1611	5,243	1.5	79
Cameroon	14,693	2,472	7,389	2.1	73
Canada	30,857	1,810	7,161	0.6	–
Cape Verde	418	60	196	–	81
Central African Rep.	3,550	563	1,751	1.6	54
Chad	7,458	1,338	3,906	2.7	44
Chile	15,019	1,448	5,082	1.1	96
China	1,266,838	97,793	380,430	0.7	91
Colombia	41,564	4,788	16,235	1.4	91
Comoros	676	106	338	–	78
Congo	2,864	525	1,513	2.6	83
Congo, Dem. Rep.	50,335	9,742	27,553	2.9	83
Costa Rica	3,933	437	1,532	1.3	95
Côte d'Ivoire	14,526	2,304	7,433	1.6	63
Croatia	4,477	235	971	−0.3	99
Cuba	11,160	732	2,857	0.3	96

Sources: Cols 1, 2 and 3: United Nations Population Division in UNICEF, *The State of the World's Children* 2001; Col 4: World Bank, World Development Indicators 2000; Cols 5 and 6: United Nations Educational, Scientific and Cultural Organization (UNESCO) in UNICEF, *The State of the World's Children* 2001.

6 ADULT FEMALE LITERACY percentages 1999	7 LIFE EXPECTANCY AT BIRTH years 1999	8 URBAN POPULATION as a percentage of total population 1999	9 GROSS NATIONAL PRODUCT (GNP) US$ per person 1999	10 GDP GENERATED BY SERVICE SECTOR percentages 1998	Countries
16	46	22	250	–	Afghanistan
–	73	41	870	21	Albania
54	69	60	1,550	41	Algeria
29	48	34	220	36	Angola
96	73	90	7,600	66	Argentina
99	71	70	490	35	Armenia
–	78	85	20,050	71	Australia
–	77	65	25,970	68	Austria
96	70	57	550	41	Azerbaijan
96	74	88	12,400	–	Bahamas
73	73	92	7,640	–	Bahrain
48	59	24	370	50	Bangladesh
97	77	49	6,610	–	Barbados
97	68	71	2,630	40	Belarus
–	77	97	24,510	71	Belgium
75	75	54	2,730	–	Belize
19	54	42	380	48	Benin
28	62	7	510	–	Bhutan
78	62	62	1,010	56	Bolivia
89	74	43	–	–	Bosnia-Herzegovina
75	45	50	3,240	50	Botswana
85	67	81	4,420	63	Brazil
85	76	72	24,630	–	Brunei
98	72	69	1,380	56	Bulgaria
10	45	18	240	39	Burkina Faso
78	61	27	220	38	Burma
27	43	9	120	29	Burundi
58	54	16	260	35	Cambodia
53	54	48	580	36	Cameroon
–	79	77	19,320	–	Canada
61	70	61	1,330	–	Cape Verde
27	45	41	290	29	Central African Rep.
22	48	24	200	46	Chad
96	75	85	4,740	62	Chile
77	70	32	780	33	China
92	71	74	2,250	61	Colombia
70	60	33	350	–	Comoros
67	49	62	670	39	Congo
54	52	30	110	25	Congo, Dem. Rep.
95	76	48	2,740	61	Costa Rica
37	47	46	710	51	Côte d'Ivoire
96	73	57	4,580	59	Croatia
96	76	75	1,170	–	Cuba

ol 7: WHO; Cols 7 and 8: United Nations Population Division in UNICEF, *The State of the World's Children* 2001; Col 9: World Bank in UNICEF, *The State of the World's Children* 001; Col 10: World Bank, World Development Indicators 2000.

WORLD TABLE

Countries	1 POPULATION thousands 1999	2 POPULATION Under 5 years old thousands 1999	3 POPULATION Under 18 years old thousands 1999	4 POPULATION GROWTH projected annual rate 1998–2015	5 ADULT MALE LITERACY percentages 1999
Cyprus	778	56	222	–	98
Czech Republic	10,262	476	2,157	-0.2	–
Denmark	5,282	324	1,105	0.0	–
Djibouti	629	98	302	–	60
Dominican Republic	8,364	944	3,306	1.3	82
Ecuador	12,411	1,465	5,063	1.5	91
Egypt	67,226	8,081	28,745	1.5	64
El Salvador	6,154	792	2,606	1.6	79
Equatorial Guinea	442	75	219	–	89
Eritrea	3,719	635	1,885	2.3	–
Estonia	1,412	62	322	-0.5	98
Ethiopia	61,095	11,032	32,108	2.1	40
Fiji	806	84	314	–	94
Finland	5,165	299	1,144	0.1	–
France	58,886	3,572	13,421	0.2	–
Gabon	1,197	190	545	2.2	74
Gambia	1,268	205	586	2.2	38
Georgia	5,006	344	1,362	-0.1	100
Germany	82,178	3,857	15,687	-0.2	–
Ghana	19,678	3,189	9,917	2.2	75
Greece	10,626	496	2,034	-0.1	98
Guatemala	11,090	1,816	5,650	2.1	74
Guinea	7,360	1,234	3,770	2.0	50
Guinea-Bissau	1,187	199	581	1.8	48
Guyana	855	87	311	–	99
Haiti	8,087	1,136	3,930	1.6	47
Honduras	6,316	966	3,094	2.1	70
Hungary	10,076	514	2,123	-0.4	100
Iceland	279	22	78	–	–
India	998,056	114,976	398,306	1.3	71
Indonesia	209,255	22,006	77,805	1.2	90
Iran	66,796	7,017	30,092	1.7	82
Iraq	22,450	3,431	10,853	2.0	71
Ireland	3,705	256	996	0.6	–
Israel	6,101	583	2,031	1.4	97
Italy	57,343	2,620	9,976	-0.3	99
Jamaica	2,560	272	959	0.9	69
Japan	126,505	6,171	23,371	-0.1	–
Jordan	6,482	1,024	3,163	2.3	93
Kazakhstan	16,269	1,415	5,494	0.3	99
Kenya	29,549	4,462	15,127	1.7	86
Kirgistan	4,669	554	1,948	1.1	99
Korea (North)	23,702	2,386	7,560	0.7	100

 Sources: Cols 1, 2 and 3: United Nations Population Division in UNICEF, *The State of the World's Children* 2001; Col 4: World Bank, World Development Indicators 2000; Cols 5 and 6: United Nations Educational, Scientific and Cultural Organization (UNESCO) in UNICEF, *The State of the World's Children* 2001.

6 ADULT FEMALE LITERACY percentages 1999	7 LIFE EXPECTANCY AT BIRTH years 1999	8 URBAN POPULATION as a percentage of total population 1999	9 GROSS NATIONAL PRODUCT (GNP) US$ per person 1999	10 GDP GENERATED BY SERVICE SECTOR percentages 1998	Countries
93	78	56	11,960	–	Cyprus
–	74	75	5,060	57	Czech Republic
–	76	85	32,030	–	Denmark
33	51	83	790	–	Djibouti
81	71	64	1,910	56	Dominican Republic
86	70	64	1,310	52	Ecuador
38	67	45	1,400	50	Egypt
73	70	46	1,900	60	El Salvador
67	51	47	1,170	–	Equatorial Guinea
10	51	18	200	61	Eritrea
98	69	69	3,480	67	Estonia
27	44	17	100	44	Ethiopia
89	73	49	2,210	–	Fiji
–	77	67	23,780	62	Finland
–	78	75	23,480	72	France
53	52	80	3,350	32	Gabon
24	48	32	340	59	Gambia
100	73	60	620	58	Georgia
–	77	87	25,350	44	Germany
53	61	38	390	83	Ghana
94	78	60	11,770	–	Greece
63	65	40	1,660	57	Guatemala
22	47	32	510	42	Guinea
16	45	23	160	25	Guinea-Bissau
97	65	38	760	–	Guyana
42	54	35	460	50	Haiti
69	70	52	760	49	Honduras
99	71	64	4,650	60	Hungary
–	79	92	29,280	–	Iceland
44	63	28	450	46	India
78	66	40	580	35	Indonesia
69	70	61	1,760	38	Iran
45	65	77	2,170	–	Iraq
–	77	59	19,160	–	Ireland
93	78	91	17450	–	Israel
98	78	67	19,710	67	Italy
81	75	56	2,330	58	Jamaica
–	80	79	32,230	61	Japan
81	71	74	1,500	71	Jordan
99	68	56	1,230	60	Kazakhstan
69	51	32	360	58	Kenya
95	68	34	300	30	Kirgistan
100	73	60	<755	–	Korea (North)

Col 7: WHO; Cols 7 and 8: United Nations Population Division in UNICEF, *The State of the World's Children* 2001; Col 9: World Bank in UNICEF, *The State of the World's Children* 2001; Col 10: World Bank, World Development Indicators 2000.

WORLD TABLE

Countries	1 POPULATION thousands 1999	2 POPULATION Under 5 years old thousands 1999	3 POPULATION Under 18 years old thousands 1999	4 POPULATION GROWTH projected annual rate 1998–2015	5 ADULT MALE LITERACY percentages 1999
Korea (South)	46,480	3,403	12,400	0.6	99
Kuwait	1,897	200	792	2.5	95
Laos	5,297	883	2,670	2.2	74
Latvia	2,389	105	547	−0.8	100
Lebanon	3,236	368	1,257	1.2	91
Lesotho	2,108	316	977	1.6	70
Liberia	2,930	475	1,515	–	36
Libya	5,471	724	2,514	2.0	87
Lithuania	3,682	193	896	−0.1	100
Luxembourg	426	26	91	–	–
Macedonia	2,011	152	567	0.4	97
Madagascar	15,497	2,706	7,814	2.7	50
Malawi	10,640	1,990	5,738	2.2	66
Malaysia	21,830	2,644	8,864	1.6	89
Maldives	278	43	141	–	98
Mali	10,960	1,997	5,868	2.7	48
Malta	386	25	97	–	90
Marshall Islands	62	9	28	–	–
Mauritania	2,598	439	1,307	2.3	60
Mauritius	1,150	94	357	0.9	86
Mexico	97,365	11,202	38,823	1.4	92
Moldova	4,380	287	1,290	−0.2	99
Mongolia	2,621	279	1,110	1.5	97
Morocco	27,867	3,215	11,030	1.4	58
Mozambique	19,286	3,414	9,893	2.0	55
Namibia	1,695	264	817	1.7	80
Nepal	23,385	3,485	11,258	2.1	63
Netherlands	15,735	925	3,412	0.2	–
New Zealand	3,828	289	1,035	0.5	–
Nicaragua	4,938	804	2,490	2.2	65
Niger	10,400	2,034	5,698	3.0	21
Nigeria	108,945	17,880	54,771	2.5	66
Norway	4,442	293	1,028	0.3	–
Oman	2,460	395	1,260	2.2	79
Pakistan	152,331	23,793	73,691	2.3	57
Panama	2,812	302	1,056	1.2	93
Papua New Guinea	4,702	668	2,127	1.8	81
Paraguay	5,358	765	2,503	1.9	93
Peru	25,230	2,898	10,174	1.5	96
Philippines	74,454	9,800	32,371	1.7	94
Poland	38,740	2,152	9,798	0.0	99
Portugal	9,873	525	2,018	−0.1	93
Qatar	589	50	182	–	84

 Sources: Cols 1, 2 and 3: United Nations Population Division in UNICEF, *The State of the World's Children* 2001; Col 4: World Bank, World Development Indicators 2000; Cols 5 and 6: United Nations Educational, Scientific and Cultural Organization (UNESCO) in UNICEF, *The State of the World's Children* 2001.

6 ADULT FEMALE LITERACY percentages 1999	7 LIFE EXPECTANCY AT BIRTH years 1999	8 URBAN POPULATION as a percentage of total population 1999	9 GROSS NATIONAL PRODUCT (GNP) US$ per person 1999	10 GDP GENERATED BY SERVICE SECTOR percentages 1998	Countries
98	73	81	8,490	52	Korea (South)
83	76	98	19,020	–	Kuwait
48	54	23	280	25	Laos
99	69	69	2,470	66	Latvia
77	70	89	3,700	61	Lebanon
92	54	27	550	47	Lesotho
18	50	45	490*	–	Liberia
67	70	87	5,540	–	Libya
99	71	68	2,620	57	Lithuania
–	77	91	44,640	–	Luxembourg
91	73	62	1,690	60	Macedonia
44	58	29	250	56	Madagascar
34	40	24	190	46	Malawi
79	72	57	3,400	43	Malaysia
99	65	26	1,160	–	Maldives
12	54	30	240	36	Mali
91	78	90	9,210	–	Malta
90	–	72	1,560	–	Marshall Islands
33	54	57	380	46	Mauritania
78	72	41	3,590	58	Mauritius
87	73	74	4,400	68	Mexico
97	68	46	370	40	Moldova
97	67	63	350	40	Mongolia
31	67	55	1,200	51	Morocco
23	42	39	230	45	Mozambique
77	48	30	1,890	56	Namibia
28	58	12	220	37	Nepal
–	78	89	24,320	–	Netherlands
–	77	86	13,780	–	New Zealand
67	68	56	430	44	Nicaragua
7	49	20	190	42	Niger
47	50	43	310	27	Nigeria
–	78	75	32,880	66	Norway
57	71	83	4,940	–	Oman
33	65	37	470	49	Pakistan
92	74	56	3,070	74	Panama
63	59	17	800	33	Papua New Guinea
90	70	55	1,580	49	Paraguay
89	69	72	2,390	56	Peru
94	69	58	1,020	51	Philippines
99	73	65	3,960	62	Poland
87	76	63	10,600	–	Portugal
81	72	92	12,000*	–	Qatar

ɔl 7: WHO; Cols 7 and 8: United Nations Population Division in UNICEF, *The State of the World's Children* 2001; Col 9: World Bank in UNICEF, *The State of the World's Children* ɔ001; Col 10: World Bank, World Development Indicators 2000.

WORLD TABLE

Countries	1 POPULATION thousands 1999	2 POPULATION Under 5 years old thousands 1999	3 POPULATION Under 18 years old thousands 1999	4 POPULATION GROWTH projected annual rate 1998-2015	5 ADULT MALE LITERACY percentages 1999
Romania	22,402	1,024	5,096	-0.3	99
Russia	147,196	7,006	34,811	-0.4	100
Rwanda	7,235	1,259	3,829	2.2	56
Saudi Arabia	20,899	3.220	9,831	2.9	91
Senegal	9,240	1,596	4,755	2.3	43
Seychelles	77	14	40	–	87
Sierra Leone	4,717	831	2,379	1.9	45
Singapore	3,522	265	914	1.0	96
Slovakia	5,382	298	1,357	0.1	–
Slovenia	1,989	93	411	-0.2	100
Solomon Islands	430	70	215	–	–
Somalia	9,672	1,957	5,269	–	36
South Africa	39,900	4,909	16,550	1.0	67
Spain	39,634	1,822	7,345	-0.2	98
Sri Lanka	18,639	1,597	6,163	1.1	92
Sudan	28,883	4,162	13,618	2.1	67
Suriname	415	40	160	–	95
Swaziland	980	161	488	–	81
Sweden	8,892	478	1,934	-0.1	–
Switzerland	7,344	414	1,539	-0.1	82
Syria	15,725	2,183	7,739	2.1	91
Tajikistan	6,104	863	2,899	1.5	93
Tanzania	32,793	5,724	17,204	2.0	87
Thailand	60,856	4,831	19,039	0.9	96
Togo	4,512	800	2,373	2.0	67
Trinidad & Tobago	1,289	91	424	0.7	–
Tunisia	9,460	924	3,563	1.2	76
Turkey	65,546	6,659	22,918	1.2	94
Turkmenistan	4,384	570	1,953	1.5	99
Uganda	21,143	4,348	12,026	2.3	74
Ukraine	50,658	2,478	11,533	-0.8	98
United Arab Emirates	2,398	212	811	1.9	85
United Kingdom	58,744	3,521	13,337	0.0	–
United States of America	276,218	19,344	71,442	0.7	–
Uruguay	3,313	283	976	0.6	96
Uzbekistan	23,942	3,061	10,674	1.4	99
Venezuela	23,706	2,791	9,660	1.5	92
Vietnam	78,705	8,454	31,926	1.2	95
Western Samoa	177	24	80	–	–
Yemen	17,488	3,479	9,540	2.8	69
Yugoslavia	10,637	668	2,659	0.0	99
Zambia	8,976	1,613	4,939	1.7	76
Zimbabwe	11,529	1,625	5,664	1.1	90

Sources: Cols 1, 2 and 3: United Nations Population Division in UNICEF, *The State of the World's Children* 2001; Col 4: World Bank, World Development Indicators 2000; Cols 5 and 6: United Nations Educational, Scientific and Cultural Organization (UNESCO) in UNICEF, *The State of the World's Children* 2001.

6 ADULT FEMALE LITERACY percentages 1999	7 LIFE EXPECTANCY AT BIRTH years 1999	8 URBAN POPULATION as a percentage of total population 1999	9 GROSS NATIONAL PRODUCT (GNP) US$ per person 1999	10 GDP GENERATED BY SERVICE SECTOR percentages 1998	Countries
96	70	56	1,520	43	Romania
99	67	77	2,270	57	Russia
50	41	6	250	31	Rwanda
70	72	85	6,910	45	Saudi Arabia
23	53	47	510	59	Senegal
89	–	62	6,540	–	Seychelles
18	39	36	130	32	Sierra Leone
86	78	100	29,610	65	Singapore
–	73	57	3,590	64	Slovakia
100	75	50	9,890	57	Slovenia
56	72	19	750	–	Solomon Islands
14	48	27	120	–	Somalia
66	52	50	3,160	64	South Africa
96	78	77	14,000	25	Spain
88	74	23	820	51	Sri Lanka
47	56	35	330	43	Sudan
91	71	74	1,660	–	Suriname
78	61	26	1,360	–	Swaziland
–	79	83	25,040	–	Sweden
80	79	68	38,350	–	Switzerland
73	69	54	970	–	Syria
88	68	28	290	65	Tajikistan
82	48	32	240	39	Tanzania
92	69	21	1,960	48	Thailand
33	49	33	320	37	Togo
99	–	74	1,720	51	Trinidad & Tobago
53	74	65	4,390	59	Tunisia
74	70	74	2,100	57	Turkey
97*	70	45	2,900	34	Turkmenistan
50	42	14	320	38	Uganda
99	69	68	750	51	Ukraine
93	75	85	17,870	–	United Arab Emirates
–	78	89	22,640	67	United Kingdom
–	77	77	30,600	72	United States of America
97	74	91	5,900	64	Uruguay
99	68	37	720	42	Uzbekistan
90	73	87	3,670	61	Venezuela
88	68	20	370	42	Vietnam
98	72	22	1,060	–	Western Samoa
36	59	25	350	34	Yemen
97	73	52	–	–	Yugoslavia
60	41	40	320	56	Zambia
82	43	35	520	56	Zimbabwe

Col 7: WHO; Cols 7 and 8: United Nations Population Division in UNICEF, *The State of the World's Children* 2001; Col 9: World Bank in UNICEF, *The State of the World's Children* 2001; Col 10: World Bank, World Development Indicators 2000.

MEDIA TABLE

Countries	1 TELEPHONE LINES per 100 people 1999 or latest available data	2 CELL PHONES per 1,000 people 1998	3 NEWSPAPERS per 100 people 1996	4 RADIO per 100 people 1997	5 TELEVISION SETS per 100 people 1998	percentage of households 1999
Afghanistan	–	–	–	12	–	–
Albania	4	1	3.6	21	109	–
Algeria	5	1	3.8	24	105	–
Angola	1	1	1.1	6	14	–
Argentina	20	78	12.3	67	289	97
Armenia	16	2	2.3	24	218	–
Australia	52	286	29.3	–	639	99
Austria	47	282	29.6	74	516	97
Azerbaijan	9	8	2.7	2	254	–
Bahamas	37	–	–	71	–	–
Bahrain	25	–	–	50	–	99
Bangladesh	0	1	0.9	5	6	–
Barbados	42	–	–	88	–	–
Belarus	26	1	17.4	29	314	98
Belgium	50	173	16.0	79	510	95
Belize	16	–	–	56	–	–
Benin	1	1	0.2	10	10	–
Bhutan	2	–	–	6	–	–
Bolivia	6	27	5.5	64	116	–
Bosnia-Herzegovina		7	15.2	24	41	–
Botswana	8	15	2.7	15	20	–
Brazil	15	47	4.0	42	316	86
Brunei	25	–	–	29	–	–
Bulgaria	34	15	25.7	54	398	94
Burkina Faso	0	0	0.1	3	9	–
Burma	1	0	1.0	9	7	28
Burundi	0	0	0.3	6	4	–
Cambodia	0	6	0.2	12	123	37
Cameroon	1	0	0.7	15	32	–
Canada	63	176	15.9	103	715	99
Cape Verde	11	–	–	17	–	–
Central African Rep.		00	0.2	8	5	–
Chad	0	0	0	22	1	–
Chile	21	65	9.8	34	232	93.4
China	9	19	–	33	272	89
Colombia	16	49	4.6	5	217	98
Comoros	1	–	–	13	–	–
Congo	1	1	0.8	12	12	–
Congo, Dem. Rep.	0	0	0.3	36	135	–
Costa Rica	20	28	9.4	25	387	80
Côte d'Ivoire	2	6	1.7	15	70	–
Croatia	36	41	11.5	34	272	90
Cuba	4	0	11.8	35	239	–

Sources: Col 1: International Telecommunications Union 2000; Cols 2 and 3: World Bank, *World Development Indicators 2000*; Col 4: International Telecommunications Union 2000; Col 5: World Bank, *World Development Indicators 2000*; Zenith 2000.

6 SATELLITE TV percentage of households 1999	7 CABLE TV percentage of households 1999	8 INTERNET HOSTS per 10,000 people 1999	8 number per country 1999	9 MOVIE THEATERS number of visits per person 1998	10 MUSIC SALES share of recorded music sales 1999	Countries
–	–	–	1	–	–	Afghanistan
–	–	0.24	215	–	–	Albania
–	–	0.01	200	–	–	Algeria
–	–	0.00	6	–	–	Angola
1.4	63.1	27.85	142,470	0.9	0.70	Argentina
–		1.85	2,313	–	–	Armenia
5	11	477.85	1,090,468	4.3	1.70	Australia
37	39.5	252.01	262,632	1.9	0.84	Austria
–	–	0.23	603	0.02	–	Azerbaijan
–	–	–	4	–	–	Bahamas
–	–	–	1,117	1.5	0.01	Bahrain
–	–	0.00	1	–	–	Bangladesh
–	–	–	68	–	–	Barbados
–	25	0.77	883	–	–	Belarus
3.6	91.2	266.90	339,357	2.3	0.89	Belgium
–	–	–	276	–	–	Belize
–	–	0.04	27	–	–	Benin
–	–	–	542	–	–	Bhutan
–	–	0.47	948	0.4	0.01	Bolivia
–	–	1.38	2,232	–	–	Bosnia-Herzegovina
–	–	6.00	2,226	–	–	Botswana
1.2	7.2	18.45	446,444	0.8	1.74	Brazil
–	–	–	1,399	–	–	Brunei
8.7	34.4	11.89	16,832	0.3	0.01	Bulgaria
–	–	0.19	211	–	–	Burkina Faso
–	–	0.00	4	–	–	Burma
–	–	0.00	1	–	–	Burundi
–	–	0.12	155	–	–	Cambodia
–	–	0.00	5	–	–	Cameroon
4	76	422.97	1,669,664	3.5	2.29	Canada
–	–	–	1	–	–	Cape Verde
–	–	0.00	7	–	–	Central African Rep.
–	–	0.00	5	–	–	Chad
0.7	17.9	21.45	40,190	0.6	0.20	Chile
–	70	0.50	71,769	0.1	0.24	China
1	40	7.51	40,565	0.6	0.29	Colombia
–	–	–	33	–	–	Comoros
–	–	0.00	3	–	–	Congo
–	–	0.00	8	–	–	Congo, Dem. Rep.
0.9	8.9	10.41	7,471	–	–	Costa Rica
–	–	0.25	629	–	–	Côte d'Ivoire
22	–	25.94	14,535	0.7	0.03	Croatia
–	–	0.06	169	–	–	Cuba

Cols 6 and 7: Zenith 2000; Col 8: World Bank, *World Development Indicators 2000*; Col 9: *Screen Digest* 2000; Col 10: ARIA 2000.

MEDIA TABLE

Countries	1 TELEPHONE LINES per 100 people 1999 or latest available data	2 CELL PHONES per 1,000 people 1998	3 NEWSPAPERS per 100 people 1996	4 RADIO per 100 people 1997	5 TELEVISION SETS per 100 people 1998	5 percentage o households 1999
Cyprus	54	–	–	40	–	–
Czech Republic	37	94	25.4	80	447	99
Denmark	68	364	30.9	113	585	97
Djibouti	1	–	–	8	–	–
Dominican Republic	9	31	5.2	17	95	78
Ecuador	9	25	7.0	40	293	58.9
Egypt	6	1	4.0	3	122	–
El Salvador	8	18	4.8	45	675	–
Equatorial Guinea	1	–	–	44	–	–
Eritrea	1	0	–	32	14	–
Estonia	35	170	17.4	70	480	96
Ethiopia	0	0	0.1	20	5	–
Fiji	10	–	–	62	–	–
Finland	55	572	45.5	148	640	97
France	58	188	21.8	94	601	96
Gabon	3	8	2.9	17	55	–
Gambia	2	4	0.2	15	3	–
Georgia	12	11	–	55	473	–
Germany	59	170	31.1	95	580	97
Ghana	1	1	1.4	22	99	–
Greece	53	194	15.3	47	466	96
Guatemala	5	10	3.3	7	126	60.6
Guinea	1	3	–	5	41	–
Guinea-Bissau	1	0	0.5	4	–	–
Guyana	7	–	–	49	–	–
Haiti	1	0	0.3	5	5	–
Honduras	4	5	5.5	39	90	–
Hong Kong	56	475	792	65	431	99
Hungary	40	105	18.6	68	437	94
Iceland	68	–	–	93	–	–
India	2	1	–	11	69	33
Indonesia	3	5	2.4	15	136	61
Iran	13	6	2.8	26	157	–
Iraq	3	0	1.9	22	83	–
Ireland	48	257	15.0	69	403	98
Israel	46	359	29.0	50	318	95
Italy	46	355	10.4	88	486	99
Jamaica	20	22	6.2	47	182	–
Japan	49	374	57.8	95	707	99
Jordan	8	12	5.8	25	52	–
Kazakhstan	11	2	–	40	231	–
Kenya	1	0	0.9	10	21	30
Kirgistan	8	0	1.5	11	45	–

 Sources: Col 1: International Telecommunications Union 2000; Cols 2 and 3: World Bank, *World Development Indicators 2000*; Col 4: International Telecommunications Union 2000; Col 5: World Bank, *World Development Indicators 2000*; Zenith 2000.

6 SATELLITE TV percentage of households 1999	7 CABLE TV percentage of households 1999	8 INTERNET HOSTS per 10,000 people 1999	 number per country 1999	9 MOVIE THEATERS number of visits per person 1998	10 MUSIC SALES share of recorded music sales 1999	Countries
–	–	–	6,225	1.2	0.05	Cyprus
12	21	85.58	122,253	0.9	0.13	Czech Republic
17	57.8	540.30	338,239	2.1	0.69	Denmark
–	–	–	40	–	–	Djibouti
–	6	7.63	6,574	0.6	–	Dominican Republic
–	10.6	1.42	1,922	0.4	0.01	Ecuador
–	–	0.28	2,355	0.3	0.14	Egypt
–	–	1.17	975	–	–	El Salvador
–	–	–	0	–	–	Equatorial Guinea
–	–	0.01	6	–	–	Eritrea
4	35	174.65	30,103	0.7	0.02	Estonia
–	–	0.01	81	–	–	Ethiopia
–	–	–	359	–	–	Fiji
6.3	35.2	1,116.78	461,760	1.2	0.33	Finland
15	12.2	110.64	1,233,071	2.9	5.15	France
–	–	0.02	2	–	–	Gabon
–	–	0.02	12	–	–	Gambia
–	–	1.59	898	–	–	Georgia
31	55	173.96	1,635,067	1.8	7.36	Germany
–	–	0.06	110	–	–	Ghana
–	8	59.57	75,088	1.2	0.26	Greece
2.9	32.9	1.26	1,772	–	–	Guatemala
–	–	0.00	1	–	–	Guinea
–	–	0.13	15	–	–	Guinea-Bissau
–	–	–	16	–	–	Guyana
–	–	0.00	1	–	–	Haiti
–	–	0.19	119	–	–	Honduras
20	24	142.77	114,882	3.4	0.26	Hong Kong
18	45.6	93.13	119,642	2.1	0.15	Hungary
–	–	–	29,872	5	0.05	Iceland
1	44	0.18	23,445	2.9	0.45	India
1	–	0.76	21,052	1.1	0.33	Indonesia
–	–	0.05	564	–	–	Iran
–	–	0.00	5	–	–	Iraq
9	44	156.68	63,913	3.4	0.29	Ireland
2	69.8	187.41	149,490	1.9	0.14	Israel
4.1	–	68.28	301,528	2.1	1.58	Italy
–	–	1.04	367	0.8	0.01	Jamaica
29	32	163.75	2,636,541	1.2	16.71	Japan
28	–	1.17	612	–	–	Jordan
–	–	1.42	3,750	–	–	Kazakhstan
0.5	0.2	0.19	602	0.5	–	Kenya
–	–	4.13	3,535	–	–	Kirgistan

ols 6 and 7: Zenith 2000; Col 8: World Bank, *World Development Indicators 2000*; Col 9: *Screen Digest* 2000; Col 10: ARIA 2000.

MEDIA TABLE

Countries	1 TELEPHONE LINES per 100 people 1999 or latest available data	2 CELL PHONES per 1,000 people 1998	3 NEWSPAPERS per 100 people 1996	4 RADIO per 100 people 1997	5 TELEVISION SETS	
					per 100 people 1998	percentage of households 1999
Korea (North)	5	0	19.9	14	53	–
Korea (South)	44	302	39.3	102	346	100
Kuwait	24	138	37.4	62	491	100
Laos	1	1	0.4	53	4	38
Latvia	30	68	24.7	72	492	98
Lebanon	19	157	10.7	88	352	99
Lesotho	1	5	0.8	5	25	–
Liberia	0	–	–	27	–	–
Libya	9	3	1.4	25	126	–
Lithuania	31	72	9.3	51	459	98
Luxembourg	72	–	–	66	–	–
Macedonia	23	15	2.1	20	250	90
Madagascar	0	1	0.5	20	21	–
Malawi	0	1	0.3	24	2	–
Malaysia	20	99	15.8	42	166	97
Mali	0	0	0.1	5	12	–
Malta	51	–	–	66	–	–
Marshall Islands	6	–	–	–	––	–
Mauritania	1	0	0	14	91	–
Mauritius	22	53	7.5	36	226	84
Mexico	11	35	9.7	32	261	96
Moldova	13	2	6.0	73	297	–
Mongolia	4	1	2.7	14	63	–
Morocco	7	4	2.6	24	160	–
Mozambique	0	0	0.3	4	5	–
Namibia	6	12	1.9	14	37	–
Nepal	1	0	1.1	3	6	–
Netherlands	61	213	30.6	96	543	98
New Zealand	49	203	21.6	98	508	98
Nicaragua	3	4	3.0	25	190	–
Niger	0	0	0	6	27	–
Nigeria	0	0	2.4	216	66	69
Norway	71	474	58.8	96	579	98
Oman	9	43	2.9	57	595	98
Pakistan	2	1	2.3	10	88	37
Panama	16	29	6.2	29	187	78.6
Papua New Guinea	–	1	1.5	9	24	–
Paraguay	6	41	4.3	17	101	–
Peru	7	30	8.4	25	144	–
Philippines	3	22	7.9	15	108	73
Poland	26	50	11.3	6	413	97
Portugal	42	309	7.5	30	542	99
Qatar	26	–	–	43	–	97

 Sources: Col 1: International Telecommunications Union 2000; Cols 2 and 3: World Bank, *World Development Indicators 2000*; Col 4: International Telecommunications Union 2000; Col 5: World Bank, *World Development Indicators 2000*; Zenith 2000.

6 SATELLITE TV percentage of households 1999	7 CABLE TV percentage of households 1999	8 INTERNET HOSTS per 10,000 people 1999	8 INTERNET HOSTS number per country 1999	9 MOVIE THEATERS number of visits per person 1998	10 MUSIC SALES share of recorded music sales 1999	Countries
–	–	–	–	–	–	Korea (North)
–	9	55.53	283,459	1.0	0.61	Korea (South)
77	–	23.76	4,069	0.3	0.02	Kuwait
0.1	–	0.00	0	–	–	Laos
3	17	50.86	18,877	0.5	0.01	Latvia
15	–	7.02	4,729	–	0.03	Lebanon
–	–	0.08	50	–	–	Lesotho
–	–	–	0	–	–	Liberia
–	–	0.00	3	–	–	Libya
2.6	18.6	30.45	14,193	0.2	0.01	Lithuania
–	–	–	9,614	3.6	–	Luxembourg
–	–	4.40	1,487	–	–	Macedonia
–	–	0.12	337	–	–	Madagascar
–	–	0.00	1	–	–	Malawi
6	–	23.53	59,012	0.7	0.14	Malaysia
–	–	0.01	11	–	–	Mali
–	–	–	6,005	–	–	Malta
–	–	–	2	–	–	Marshall Islands
–	–	0.00	59	–	–	Mauritania
–	0.1	4.56	823	–	–	Mauritius
0.9	14.2	23.02	404,873	1.1	1.63	Mexico
–	–	2.42	1,267	–	–	Moldova
–	–	0.04	50	–	–	Mongolia
–	–	0.28	2,034	0.6	–	Morocco
–	–	0.09	162	–	–	Mozambique
–	–	11.73	2,043	–	–	Namibia
–	–	0.07	290	–	–	Nepal
4	94	403.49	959,083	1.3	1.36	Netherlands
6	28	476.18	271,003	4.4	0.26	New Zealand
–	–	2.21	1,028	–	–	Nicaragua
–	–	0.03	32	–	–	Niger
15	7	0.00	77	–	–	Nigeria
20	42	754.15	438,961	2.6	0.68	Norway
72	–	2.87	678	–	0.01	Oman
13	5	0.22	4,735	0.08	0.02	Pakistan
2	10	2.97	1,235	3.4	–	Panama
–	–	0.49	337	–	–	Papua New Guinea
–	–	2.43	1,660	0.07	0.01	Paraguay
–	–	3.09	9,230	0.2	0.04	Peru
3	10	1.29	12,394	1.5	0.12	Philippines
17	35	40.86	171,217	0.5	0.40	Poland
8.4	20	59.40	77,761	1.4	0.46	Portugal
28	–	–	31	0.6	0.01	Qatar

Cols 6 and 7: Zenith 2000; Col 8: World Bank, *World Development Indicators 2000*; Col 9: *Screen Digest* 2000; Col 10: ARIA 2000.

MEDIA TABLE

Countries	1 TELEPHONE LINES per 100 people 1999 or latest available data	2 CELL PHONES per 1,000 people 1998	3 NEWSPAPERS per 100 people 1996	4 RADIO per 100 people 1997	5 TELEVISION SETS per 100 people 1998	percentage of households 1999
Romania	17	29	30.0	32	233	87
Russia	20	5	10.5	42	420	99
Rwanda	0	1	0	8	0	–
Saudi Arabia	14	31	5.7	30	262	100
Senegal	2	2	0.5	13	41	–
Seychelles	25	–	–	55	–	–
Sierra Leone	0	0	0.4	23	13	–
Singapore	58	346	36.0	79	348	99
Slovakia	31	87	18.5	96	402	–
Slovenia	38	84	19.9	40	356	–
Solomon Islands	2	–	–	13	–	–
Somalia	0	–	–	5	–	–
South Africa	14	56	3.2	34	125	75
Spain	42	179	10.0	33	506	100
Sri Lanka	3	9	2.9	20	92	–
Sudan	1	0	2.7	26	87	–
Suriname	17	–	–	72	–	–
Swaziland	3	–	–	16	–	–
Sweden	66	464	44.5	93	531	100
Switzerland	70	235	33.7	99	535	93
Syria	10	0	2.0	26	70	–
Taiwan	54	–	–	35	–	99
Tajikistan	4	0	2.0	14	285	–
Tanzania	0	1	0.4	27	21	50
Thailand	8	32	6.3	23	236	94
Togo	1	2	0.4	22	18	–
Trinidad & Tobago	21	20	12.3	52	334	99
Tunisia	9	4	3.1	14	198	–
Turkey	26	53	11.1	16	286	96
Turkmenistan	8	1	–	28	201	–
Uganda	0	1	0.2	12	27	–
Ukraine	19	2	5.4	89	490	97
United Arab Emirates	41	210	15.6	34	294	98
United Kingdom	56	252	32.9	143	645	97
United States	66	256	21.5	208	847	98.1
Uruguay	27	60	29.3	59	241	98
Uzbekistan	7	1	0.3	45	275	–
Venezuela	11	87	20.6	45	185	96
Vietnam	3	2	0.4	10	47	50
Yemen	2	1	1.5	6	29	–
Yugoslavia	21	23	10.7	30	259	–
Zambia	22	1	1.2	16	137	64
Zimbabwe	1	4	1.9	39	30	82

 Sources: Col 1: International Telecommunications Union 2000; Cols 2 and 3: World Bank, *World Development Indicators 2000*; Col 4: International Telecommunications Union 2000; Col 5: World Bank, *World Development Indicators 2000*; Zenith 2000.

6 SATELLITE TV percentage of households 1999	7 CABLE TV percentage of households 1999	8 INTERNET HOSTS per 10,000 people 1999	number per country 1999	9 MOVIE THEATERS number of visits per person 1998	10 MUSIC SALES share of recorded music sales 1999	Countries
3.5	45	9.01	36,294	0.3	0.03	Romania
0.6	11.1	13.06	91,430	0.3	0.40	Russia
–	–	0.00	259	–	–	Rwanda
61	–	1.17	2,828	–	0.13	Saudi Arabia
–	–	0.28	306	–	–	Senegal
–	–	–	2	–	–	Seychelles
–	–	0.14	75	–	–	Sierra Leone
–	95	322.30	148,249	4.7	0.12	Singapore
–	–	38.79	28,183	1.1	0.03	Slovakia
–	–	99.34	23,559	1.4	0.05	Slovenia
–	–	–	210	–	–	Solomon Islands
–	–	–	2	–	–	Somalia
4.9	–	33.36	167,635	0.7	0.47	South Africa
9.1	4	76.75	469,587	2.7	1.66	Spain
–	–	0.52	1,209	–	–	Sri Lanka
–	–	0.00	0	–	–	Sudan
–	–	–	0	–	–	Suriname
–	–	–	661	–	–	Swaziland
20	42	581.47	522,888	1.8	0.93	Sweden
5	76	371.37	269,812	2.2	0.72	Switzerland
–	–	0.00	1	–	–	Syria
1	80	–	597,036	1.2	0.80	Taiwan
–	–	0.24	221	–	–	Tajikistan
2	1.5	0.05	218	–	–	Tanzania
0.5	2	4.49	40,176	0.4	0.33	Thailand
–	–	0.17	120	–	–	Togo
3	35	28.20	4,852	1.1	–	Trinidad & Tobago
–	–	0.06	33	–	–	Tunisia
6.2	5.9	8.06	78,878	0.3	0.33	Turkey
–	–	0.56	444	–	–	Turkmenistan
–	–	0.06	139	–	–	Uganda
–	–	4.56	28,973	–	0.04	Ukraine
75	–	39.44	19,718	–	0.10	United Arab Emirates
17	14	270.60	1,739,078	2.3	7.55	United Kingdom
12	76	1,508.77	53,175,956	5.4	37.01	United States
3	35	38.34	25,385	0.8	0.03	Uruguay
–	–	0.05	200	–	–	Uzbekistan
2	15	3.98	14,281	0.04	0.14	Venezuela
–	–	0.00	126	–	–	Vietnam
–	–	0.02	28	–	–	Yemen
–	–	7.65	10,544	0.5	–	Yugoslavia
–	–	–	–	–	–	Zambia
–	1.1	0.48	537	–	–	Zambia
4.7	–	1.19	2,073	–	0.03	Zimbabwe

Cols 6 and 7: Zenith 2000; Col 8: World Bank, *World Development Indicators 2000*; Col 9: *Screen Digest* 2000; Col 10: ARIA 2000.

Glossary

Affiliate – A television station that carries a network's programs in return for a fee.

Analog – A continuous varying signal or wave, which tends to be susceptible to interference.

Audience rating – The number of people or households tuned to a specific station or network as a percentage of the total number of TV households. The combined audience rating during a specific time period provides an estimate of the total number of homes actually watching television (HUTs), or people listening to the radio (PURs).

Audience share – The percentage of Homes Using Television (HUTs) or Persons Using Radio (PURs) that are tuned to a specific station or network.

Bandwidth – The measure of capacity of communications media. The greater the capacity, the greater the amount of information that can be carried.

Broadband – A term used to describe large-capacity networks that carry several services at the same time (data, voice and video). Traditional telephone networks are often described as "narrowband".

Cable television – A co-axial, wired, system for the broadcasting of programs. In the mid-1970s, satellite delivery of signals to cable systems added more stations than terrestrial broadcasters were able to deliver.

Cell – The geographic area covered by a single base station in a cellular mobile network.

Cellular service – A mobile telephone service provided by a network of base stations that cover one geographic cell within the total cellular system service area.

Cookies – Lines of text that form part of an http transaction. They were originally designed to help people navigate the web. Cookies help your computer to retrieve information over the Internet, and other people to track what you are doing. You can delete cookies on your disk and set your system to refuse cookies, but if you set your browser to reject all cookies, then you may be unable to use certain sites properly.

Cybersquatting – The registeration of the names of well-known companies as domain names, with the intention of selling the names back to the companies. Panasonic, Hertz and Avon are just some of the "victims" of cybersquatters. In the USA you can sue to get back your domain name, under a 1999 federal law known as the Anti-Cybersquatting Consumer Protection Act.

DBS (Direct Broadcast Satellite) – High-powered satellite signals transmitted directly to homes with special receiving devices. First launched in the mid-1990s, they provide Direct-to-Home (DTH) services.

DVD (Digital Versatile Disk) – An electronic storage device, similar to a CD-Rom, but with much more space. DVDs were developed for large-capacity gigabyte storage of video and other data.

Digital signal – A signal that takes on a "0" or a "1". It requires less power but more "bandwidth" than an analog signal. Digital signals can be copied precisely.

Digital Audio Broadcasting (DAB) – Radio broadcasting that uses digital signals instead of analog to improve sound quality. DAB is still growing as a service and promises to expand beyond improved FM.

Domain name – A name that identifies one or more IP addresses, and is used in URLs to identify web pages. In the URL <http://www.myriadeditions.com> the domain name is myriadeditions.com. Some common domains are <.com> (commercial), <.co> (company), <.ac> (academic), <.gov> (government). Countries can also have a domain designation.

Domain name system (DNS) – A data-query service that maps Internet addresses.

Email – Electronic mail.

Encryption – Signal scrambling so that the code can be broken only by paying subscribers.

Fixed line – A physical line connecting a subscriber to a telephone exchange. This fixed-line network is known as the PSTN.

Footprint – The area covered by a satellite signal.

HDTV (High Definition Television) – Any television system that provides an improvement in an existing system. Modern HDTV systems offer more than 1,000 scan lines with superior colour and sound.

HTML (HyperText Markup Language) – The computer code used to create hypertext documents, allowing links from one document to another.

http (HyperText Transfer Protocol) – The first part of an address (URL) of an Internet site signifying a document written in HTML.

Hyperlink – An electronic link from one web document to another. Hyperlinks are an essential part of hypertext systems, including the World Wide Web.

Internet – The Internet is the largest inter-networking system of computers in the world. It supports communications using the Transmission Control Protocol/Internet Protocol.

Internet host – A domain name that has an IP address record associated with it, i.e. any computer system that is connected to the Internet. Surveys of Internet hosts used to count the number of domain names that had IP addresses assigned to them. By 1997 the Domain Survey was not able to count a large proportion of hosts in the domain system because of organizational restrictions to domain information. The new domain survey, used by organizations such as the Internet Software Consortium (ISC) and its associates, counts the number of IP addresses that have been assigned a name.

Internet Protocol (IP) – An addressing scheme on the Internet used in combination with Transport Control Protocol (TCP). The TCP establishes the connection between two hosts.

ISDN (Intergrated Services Digital Network) – A switching system synchronized to send signals in digital form, increasing capacity over analog networks.

ISP (Internet Service Provider) – An organization that provides end-users and other ISPs access to the Internet. ISPs may also offer their own proprietary content and access to online services such as email.

JPEG (Joint Photographic Experts Group) – The digital compression standard for still images, part of the International Organization of Standardization.

Local loop – The system used to connect a telephone subscriber to the nearest switch. It normally involves a pair of copper wires, but it may also use fiber-optic or wireless technologies.

MMDS (Multi-channel, Multipoing Distribution System) – A system using microwaves to send signals instead of co-axial cable used in traditional cable television.

Modem (MOdulator-DEModulator) – A device transmitting a computer digital signal over an analog (telephone) network.

MPEG (Moving Pictures Expert Group) – A committee formed by the International Organization of Standardization (ISO) to set standards for full-motion video compression. MPEG-1 is the standard for compression of VHS quality full-motion video, and MPEG 2 for broadcast quality.

PCN (Personal Communications Networks) – PCNs are similar to Personal Communications Services, digital cellular telephone services, but provide a wider variety of voice, data and fax applications. The more "broadband" the society becomes the more PCNs you are likely to see.

POTS (Plain Old Telephone Service) – The traditional telephone allowing voice communication between two people.

Secure server – A server that uses any of the major security protocols that encrypt messages to protect them against tampering. Making purchases from a secure Web server means that a user's payment or personal information can be translated into a secret code that is difficult to decode.

Server – A computer or a device on a network that manages the network resources. There are various types of services to manage resources, including fileservers, printer servers, network servers and database servers.

Streaming – Software that supports transmissions of real-time, live or pre-recorded audio and video.

URL (Uniform Resource Locator) – The address for a specific page on the Internet. Every page has its own URL.

Video game – Games that can be played on computers or via the television set using a play-station device.

WAP (Wireless Application Protocol) phone – A world standard for wireless information and telephony services on digital mobile phones and other wireless devices developed by the Wireless Application Protocol (WAP) Forum™. It enables mobile users of wireless devices to access Internet services such as email, call management, unified messaging, weather and traffic alerts, news, sports and information services, electronic commerce transactions and banking services, online address book and directory services.

Website – A site (location) on the World Wide Web. A website contains a home page and it may also contain additional documents.

World Wide Web (www) – A hypertext-based information system that allows Internet users to create, edit or browse hypertext documents. The Web was created by CERN, the European nuclear research facility in Switzerland.

REFERENCES

Part One THE INFORMATION AGE

11 *World Telecommunication Indicators*,
International Telecommunications Union,1999

12–15 THE INFORMATION SOCIETY

SERVICE SECTOR
World Development Indicators, 2000,
<www.worldbank.org> Table 4.2
Labour Statistics Database, International
Labour Organisation, 1999

EMPLOYMENT STRUCTURE IN USA
OECD/ILO

TELEVISION RECEIVERS
Unesco Institute for Statistics, 2000

TOP SECTORS TO RECEIVE VENTURE DOLLARS
Venture Economics Information Services/NVCA

WHO IS ENCOURAGING TELEWORKING?
SHRM Benefits Survey, Society for Human
Resource Management, Alexandria, Virginia,
USA, 1999

16–17 ACCESS TO IDEAS

LITERACY
The State of the World's Children 2001,
Unicef 2001

ACCESS TO PUBLIC LIBRARIES
Unesco, 1999

ONLINE POPULATION
Unesco, 2000

ACCESS TO INTERNET FROM SCHOOLS
Ipsus Reed, 2000

18–19 E-COMMERCE

Lyn Margherio et al, *The Emerging Digital
Economy*, US Department of Commerce
<www.ecommerce.gov>
Australian Bureau of Statistics
<www.noie.gov.au>
Taylor Nelson Sofres: *B2C in Taiwan*, Taiwan,
2000
Accenture, 2000

WHY BANKS LIKE INTERNET DELIVERY
Lyn Margherio et al

CHANGING BALANCE OF E-COMMERCE
Forrester Research cited by
<www.nua.ie./surveys> November 2000

SECURE SERVERS
<www.noie.gove.au>

EUROPEAN CONSUMER SPENDING AT
E-COMMERCE SITES
Datamonitor <www.nua.ie>

WHAT DO PEOPLE PURCHASE ONLINE?
Forrester Research

Part Two THE PRESS AND RADIO

21 *World Press Trends*, 2000

22–23 NEWSPAPER CIRCULATION

NUMBER OF DAILY NEWSPAPERS
World Development Indicators, 2000
<www.worldbank.org>

CIRCULATION OF MAJOR NEWSPAPERS
WORLDWIDE
<jin.jcic.or.jp/stat>

CHANGING CIRCULATIONS
Unesco, 1999

24-25 Newspapers Online

READERSHIP DECLINE
<www.naa.org> 2000

CHANGING FORTUNES
Associated Newspapers, 2000

CONSUMPTION OF ONLINE NEWS
<www.people-press.org> 2000

26–27 LIBERTY OF THE PRESS

PRESS FREEDOM WORLDWIDE/PRESS
FREEDOM BY REGION/ CHANGES IN PRESS
FREEDOM/ TRENDS IN PRESS FREEDOM
Freedom House/Reporters Sans
Frontières/International Press Institute

DEGREES OF PRESS FREEDOM AROUND THE
  WORLD
Freedom House/Reporters Sans
  Frontières/International Press Institute

NUMBER OF JOURNALISTS IMPRISONED
NUMBER OF JOURNALISTS KILLED
International Press Institute

30–31 RADIO

David Hutchinson, *Media Policy: An
  Introduction*, Blackwell, Oxford, 1998
David Hendy, *Radio in the Global Age*, Polity,
  Cambridge UK, 2000
Stephen Barnard, *Studying Radio*, Arnold,
  London, 2000
Mia Lindgren, "Digital Broadcasting" Paper
  given at the NEMBC National Conference,
  Perth, December 10–12, 1999
<wmbr.mit.edu/cgi-bin/nation?<code=bj> now
  linked to: <www.radio-locator.com/>
<www.worlddab.org/whatis.htm>

RADIOS
International Telecommunications Union, *World
  Telecommunication Indicators 1999*

ONLINE RADIO IN USA/ONLINE RADIO
MIT

Part Three CINEMA

33 *Screen Digest*, January 2001

34–35 FALL AND RISE OF THE BIG SCREEN

Screen Digest, 2000

36–37 HOLLYWOOD
Motion Picture Association of America
Jeremy Rifkin, *The Age of Access: How the
  Shift from Ownership to Access is
  Transforming Capitalism*, London, Penguin
  Books, 2000
Janet Wasko, *Hollywood in the Information Age*,
  Polity 1994

OVERSEAS EARNINGS BY HOLLYWOOD
  DISTRIBUTORS
Variety

38–39 FORTRESS EUROPE

Janet Wasko, *Hollywood in the Information Age*,
  Polity 1994

TOP TEN: HOLLYWOOD V EUROPE
Zenith Media, 2000

MARKET SHARE/ DISTRIBUTION DOMINATION
SINGLE *v* MULTIPLE SCREENS
Media Salles

40–41 THE SILVER SCREEN

Janet Wasko, *Hollywood in the Information Age*,
  Polity 1994
Peter Biskind, *Easy Riders, Raging Bulls*,
  London, Bloomsbury, 1999

SCREEN DENSITY
Screen Digest/Unesco

RELEASE OF GLADIATOR
BFI, *Sight and Sound Mediawatch 2000*
Screen Daily <www.screendaily.com>
<www.imdb.com>

42–43 THE MOVIEGOERS

GOING TO THE MOVIES
Screen Digest, 2000

CINEMA ADMISSIONS IN THE UK
BFI, *Sight and Sound Mediawatch 2000*
Cinema Advertising Association, UK, 2001

TRENDS IN CINEMA ATTENDANCE BY REGION
Screen Digest, 2000

Part Four TELEVISION AND BEYOND

45 *Screen Digest*, November 2000

46–47 TELEVISION WORLDWIDE

Screen Digest 1999 <www.screendigest.com>
*World Communication and Information Report
  1999–2000*, Unesco, 2000
<indiantelevision.com>
John Sinclair and Mark Harrison,
  "Globalisation. The Nation and Television in
  Asia: the cases of Indian and China", Mt
  Tamborine, December 2000
Zenith Media <www.zenithmedia.com>

TELEVISION OWNERSHIP
Zenith Media, 2000

CHILDREN AND TELEVISION
Unesco, 2000
Special issue of *European Journal of Communication*, vol. 13, no. 4, December 1998
<www.psych.lse.ac.uk/young_people>

ACCESS TO CABLE TV IN CHINA
Qin Lian, *Wired China's Television: challenge and opportunity*, Financial Bureau of Lanfang, Hebei, 2000

48–49 LOCAL *v* GLOBAL, PUBLIC *v* COMMERCIAL

Zenith Media <www.zenithmedia.com>
Steve Vizard "Television Past and Present", *UQ*, 2000.
Encore, vol. 18, issue 11, December 2000
<www.media-awareness.ca>
Annenberg Public Policy Centre, June 2000
Aaron Koh, "National Education in Singapore: A Situated Response to Globalisation", CUHK, June 2000
Albert Moran, *Copycat TV: Globalisation, Program Formats and Cultural Identity*, University of Luton Press, 1998
Screen Digest <www.screendigest.com>

TV IN AUSTRALIA
Encore Magazine: The Production Magazine, December 2000

TV IN INDIA
<indiantelevision.com>

TV IN EUROPE
Screen Digest, September 1999

50–51 CABLE *v* SATELLITE

"Iran retains ban on satellite TV", United Press International, May 20, 1999, p.1008139 u.2885
"Satellite TV comes down to earth", *Business Week*, April 12, 1999 issue 3624 p.30(1)
Khalid Marghalani, Philip Palmgreen, Douglas A Boyd, "The utilization of direct satellite broadcasting (DBS) in Saudi Arabia", *Journal of Broadcasting & Electronic Media*, Summer 1998, vol.42, no.3, p.297(18)
Screen Digest <www.screendigest.com>
Zenith Media <www.zenithmedia.com>

SATELLITE TV
CABLE TV
Zenith Media, 2000

CABLE TV REVENUE IN EASTERN EUROPE
SATELLITE TV SUBSCRIBERS IN INDIA
Screen Digest, November 2000

52–53 DIGITAL TV

Jupiter Communications, 2000

PROJECTED INCREASE IN HOUSEHOLDS WITH DIGITAL TV
Screen Digest, 2000: Digital Terrestial Television – Executive Summary

54–55 TV RATINGS

"Business: Whatever happened to WebTV?"
The Economist; London, September 16, 2000, 356 (8188), p.75
J Cooper, "A wealth of viewers", *Mediaweek*, Feb 14, 2000, 8B
European Media Survey (EMS)
C Murphy, "How British TV is winning a world audience", *Marketing*, June 22, 2000, p.19
Screen Digest <www.screendigest.com>

CNN IN EUROPE
EUROSPORT IN EUROPE
European Media Survey (EMS)

US PAY-PER-VIEW REVENUE
Screen Digest, December 2000

TOP TV EXPORTERS
"Leading TV Exporters 1998", *Broadcasting & Cable's TV International*, vol.7, issue 24, p.3, 1999

56–57 HOME ENTERTAINMENT

J Schaeffler, "Year-over-Year Growth Sustains Another Record Month for DBS", *Satellite News*, vol.23, issue 24, p.1, June 2000
T K Arnold, "2000 year-end review", *Video Store*, pp.6–13, December 24–30, 2000
Screen Digest, December 2000, <screendigest.com>
Reuters, January 31, 2001

VCR SALES
INCREASE IN DVD SALES
Euromonitor, 2000

Part Five OWNERSHIP AND CONTROL

59 Majid Tehranian, *Global Communications and World Politics: Domination, Development and Discourse*, Boulder, Riener Iseas, 1999

60-61 MEDIA MOGULS

Wright Investors' Service: Corporate Information, 2000

Columbia Journalism Review 2000 <www.cjr.org/owners>

Anne Austin, Jonathan Barnard, Kate Harrad, Adam Smith and Steven Vass, *Top North American Media Owners 2000*, London, Zenith Media

Nicholas Garnham, *Emancipation, the Media and Modernity: Arguments about the Media and Social Theory*, Oxford, Oxford University Press, 2000

Jeremy Rifkin, *The Age of Access: How the Shift from Ownership to Access is Transforming Capitalism*, London, Penguin Books, 2000

Janet Wasko, *Hollywood in the Information Age*, Polity 1994

62-63 AOL TIME WARNER

Anne Austin, Jonathan Barnard, Kate Harrad, Adam Smith and Steven Vass, *Top North American Media Owners*, London, Zenith Media, 2000

THE BOTTOM LINE
Zenith Media 2000

WHEN WORLDS CONVERGE
REVENUE DISTRIBUTION
BFI, *Sight and Sound Mediawatch 2000*
Screen Daily <www.screendaily.com>
<www.imdb.com>

64-65 DISNEY

Columbia Journalism Review 2000 <www.cjr.org/owners>

Anne Austin, Jonathan Barnard, Kate Harrad, Adam Smith and Steven Vass, *Top North American Media Owners 2000*, London, Zenith Media

Jeremy Rifkin, *The Age of Access: How the Shift from Ownership to Access is Transforming Capitalism*, London, Penguin Books, 2000

Janet Wasko, *Hollywood in the Information Age*, Polity 1994

THE BOTTOM LINE
Zenith Media <www.zenithmedia.com> 2000

HOW THE DISNEY COOKIE CRUMBLES
Wright Investors' Service: Corporate Information, 2000

Anne Austin, Jonathan Barnard, Kate Harrad, Adam Smith and Steven Vass, *Top North American Media Owners 2000*, London, Zenith Media

66-67 NEWS CORPORATION

Richard Collins and Christina Murroni, *New Media, New Policies*, Polity Press, 1996

Jeremy Rifkin, *The Age of Access: How the Shift from Ownership to Access is Transforming Capitalism*, London: Penguin Books, 2000

Columbia Journalism Review 2000 <www.cjr.org/owners>

NEWS CORPORATION HOLDINGS
Wright Investors' Service: Corporate Information, 2000

REVENUE BREAKDOWN
THE AMERICANIZATION OF NEWS CORPORATION
Janet Wasko, *Hollywood in the Information Age*, 1994

Part Six ADVERTISING

69 *Sight and Sound, Mediawatch*, 2000

70-71 THE ADVERTISING INDUSTRY

ADVERTISING IN THE USA
IAB/PwC

KIDS ONLINE IN 2001 AND 2005
Computer Economics, April 22, 1999

TOP TEN WEBSITES FOR CHILDREN
Media Metrix, February 18, 1999

72–73 ADVERTISING EXPENDITURE

NTC Publications Ltd

75–75 ADVERTISING STANDARDS

MEDIA TOLERANCE
SPECIFIC RESTRICTIONS
International Advertising Association, *Sexism and Decency, Government Regulation and Industry Self-Regulation in 47 Countries,* 1989. Updated by Mark Balnaves, 2000

TV ADS AND CHILDREN
S Bildake, "Survey results used in fight to resist restrictions on ads", *Advertising Age International,* June 2000

Part Seven INFORMATION AND COMMUNICATION TECHNOLOGIES

77 Nielsen/Net Ratings, January 2001

78–79 PLAIN OLD TELEPHONE SYSTEMS
International Telecommunications Union, *World Telecommunication Indicators,* 1999

80–81 CELL PHONES

A Wooldridge, "Survey: Telecommunications: In search of smart phones", *The Economist,* London, 353 (8140) S12–S16, Oct 9, 1999

A Wooldridge, "The world in your pocket" *The Economist,* London, 353 (8140), S5–S6, Oct 9, 1999
Carl H Marcussen, "Mobile Phones, WAP and the Internet: The European Market and Usage Rates in a Global Perspective 2000–2003", October 22, 2000 <www.rcb.dk/uk/staff/chm/wap.htm>

The Independent, London, January 23, 2001
The Guardian, London, January 24, 2001, p.11

CELL PHONES
World Development Indicators, 2000

CELL PHONE SALES
MOBILE MARKETS
Euromonitor, 2000

82–83 TELCOS

FIXED-LINE NETWORK
CELL-PHONE NETWORK
OECD, 2001

COUNTRIES STILL BUNDLED
E deBony, "Telecom deregulation fails to lower rates", *InfoWorld,* vol.21, i.51, p.42B.

GLOBAL TELECOM IMBALANCE
World Telecommunications Development Report, 1998

84–85 INTERNET CONNECTIONS

NUMBER OF INTERNET HOSTS
International Telecommunications Union, *World Telecommunication Indicators,* 1999

GROWTH OF INTERNET HOSTS WORLDWIDE
TOP INTERNET USERS
Internet Software Consortium <www.isc.org>

86–87 INTERNET REGULATION

MAJOR TYPES OF INTERNET FRAUD
Internet Fraud Complaints Center, 2000

STATE RESTRAINTS ON INTERNET ACCESS
Reporters Sans Frontières, 2000

88–89 ELECTRONIC MAIL

<www.anu.edu.acu/people/Roger.Clarke>
IDC Research
<www.messagingonline.com>

FAX MACHINES
World Development Indicators, 2000

MAILBOX GROWTH
MAILBOX DISTRIBUTION
<www.messagingonline.com>

90–91 WEBSITES

Michael Dahn, "Counting Angels on a Pinhead: Critically Interpreting Web Size Estimates", *ONLINE,* January 2000 <www.onlineinc.com/onlinemag>
Anne Clyde et al: <www.hi.isl>
<www.searchenginewatch.com>
Greg R. Notess, Search Engine Showdown <www.notess.com/search>
Steve Lawrence and C. Lee Giles, "Searching the

World Wide Web," *Science* 280, no.5360 (1998), pp.98–100. www.neci.nj.nec.com>
<www.netcraft.com>
Alexander Halavais, "National borders on the world wide web", N*ew Media and Society*, vol.2(1) 7-28, (2000) pp.7–28
Gartner Advisory Group, December 20, 2000
CNET "Asia: 188 million internet users by 2004" <internetindicators.com/global.html>

FOREIGN LINKS
FOREIGN LINKS PER TOPIC
Halavais, 2000

SEARCH ENGINES
Greg R Notess, 2001

WHAT'S ON WEBSITES
<www.netcraft.com>

Part Eight GLOBAL VILLAGE, GLOBAL MARKET

93 Tain-dow Lee "The Globalization of Transnational Media", paper submitted to Stephanie Hemelryk Donald, Michael Keane and Yin Hong (eds) *Media in China: Content, Consumption and Change*, Curzon 2001

94–95 E-TOURISM

WORLD TOURISM
AVERAGE NUMBER OF VACATION DAYS
<www.anitesystems.com> November 2000
<www.tia.org/ivis/worldtourism.asp> November 2000

PROJECTED INCREASE IN E-TRAVEL BY EUROPEANS
<www.nua.ie/surveys> November 2000

TOP TEN UNESCO WORLD HERITAGE SITES
<www.unesco.org/whc/heritage.htm>

WHAT ONLINE MUSEUMS OFFER THE BROWSER
Museum Documentation Service
<www.open.gov.uk>

96–97 WORLD MUSIC

ARIA at <www.aria.com.au>
<www.ifpi.org> November 2000
<news.mp3.com/news/liststory> November 2000

COUNTRIES' SHARE OF TOTAL SALES OF RECORDED MUSIC
ARIA, 2000

TOP MUSIC WEBSITES
Media Metrix, November 2000
<mediametrix.com>

SALES OF RECORDED MUSIC
ARIA, 2000

98–99 WOMEN AND MEDIA

<wif.org/home/tvexec/index.html>
November 2000

WOMEN'S MAGAZINES
AD SPEND ON TV HOUSEWIFE
Zenith Media 2000 <www.zenithmedia.com>

WOMEN AS INTERNET USERS
<cyberatlas.internet.com>
<www.nielsen-netratings.com>

100–101 KIDS' STUFF

Richard de Cordova, "The Mickey in Macy's Window' in Eric Smoodin (ed) *Disney Discourse: Producing the Magic Kingdom*, Routledge 1994
The Media Beat, <www.comminit.com>
<www.fair.org>
<www.nopres.co.uk>

PARENTS' WISH LIST
<www.childresearch.net>

ETHNIC REPRESENTATION ON TV
POSITIVE PRESENTATIONS ON TV
<www.childrennow.org>

KIDS' TV IN ASIA
Anura Goonasekera, "Multimedia for Edutainment of Children in Asia"

INDEX

Figures in **bold** indicate a map, chart or graph. Only countries mentioned in text are indexed.